THE LIVING FLAME OF LOVE
Saint John of the Cross

THE LIVING FLAME OF LOVE
Saint John of the Cross

Modern English Version
with Notes

John Venard OCD

E.J. DWYER

First published 1990 by
E. J. Dwyer (Australia) Pty Ltd
Unit 3, 32-72 Alice Street
Newtown NSW 2042
Australia
Reprinted 1992

National Library of Australia
Cataloguing-in-Publication data

John, of the Cross, Saint, 1542-1591.
  [Llama de amor viva. English]. The living flame of love.
  Modern English version with notes.
  ISBN 0 85574 220 8.

  1. John, of the Cross, Saint, 1542–1591. Llama de amor viva. 2. Mystical
  union. I. Venard, John. II. Title.

861.3

Cover designed by Luc Oechslin
Typeset in 10/11 pt Cheltenham by Midland Typesetters, Maryborough
Printed in Singapore by Chong Moh Offset Printing Pte. Ltd

CONTENTS

INTRODUCTION

The Living Flame of Love of St. John of the Cross is a poem of four stanzas, with a prose commentary on each stanza. The first version, or redaction, was written about 1584 for Doña Ana de Penalosa, a great friend and benefactress of the Discalced Carmelite Order. The Saint was then Vicar-Provincial of Andalusia. The Second Redaction, with additions and emendations—and a rather longer version than the first—is used in this book. It must have been completed a few weeks before the Saint's death, in 1591 (the date 1584, given in the Prologue, refers to the First Redaction). It is, as it were, his last will and testament, and is all the more precious because of that.

It seems that during the last years of his life John was revising and re-editing *The Spiritual Canticle*, to which *The Living Flame* is a sequel—a continuation and elaboration of the same theme. In the Prologue to *The Living Flame* he writes: ". . . although in the stanzas we have already commented on [in *The Canticle*] we speak of the highest degree of perfection one can reach in this life, transformation in God, these stanzas [of *The Living Flame*] treat of a love within this very transformation that has a deeper quality and is more perfect."

He does not hesitate to say that "the operations of the soul thus united with God are of the divine Spirit and are divine" (*Living Flame* I.9). The soul is now so totally transformed in love's fire that it becomes like the log of wood which becomes the very fire itself, flaring up and shooting forth one single living flame. It is habitually united to God, and there are moments and times of intense actual union. All the faculties, the intellect, memory and will, and all the affections, emotions, senses, desires, appetites, and all its energy now incline to God in their first movements. All its activity is divine, in perfect freedom of heart. In the Saint's words, it is "singularly close to beatitude."

A sublime state indeed; but St. John insists that we should not be amazed or marvel at the wonders wrought by God in the soul disposed to receive the action of the Holy Spirit. Commenting on John 14.23, he says: "There is no reason to be amazed at God's granting such sublime gifts to those He determines to favor. If we consider that He is God and that He bestows them as God, with infinite love and goodness, it does not seem unreasonable" (Prologue 2). Yet "if these things are not read with the simplicity of the spirit of knowledge and love they contain, they will seem to be absurd, not reasonable" (*Spiritual Canticle*, Prologue). Only those who are "purified, cleansed, aflame with love" can accept the "language of God" (*Living Flame* I.5).

The four stanzas of the poem do not mark out a time sequence or progressive stages of union; rather they treat of different aspects of that union with the divine.

Stanza I discusses the fusion of the soul with God through the action of the Holy Spirit. The soul, assailed by the delicate, living flame, which is the Holy Spirit, becomes itself one single living flame with the Spirit of God. It longs for the Holy Spirit to "tear the veil" of this mortal life and give it perfect, lasting glory of beatitude. The sublime graces of union are a "feast of the Holy Spirit in the soul's innermost being". This "copiousness and abundance of glory of which we are conscious is a communication of the Holy Spirit" (I.9, 14). The soul simply receives: ". . . all its acts are divine—they are carried up and absorbed in the flame of the Holy Spirit, who performs the acts of the soul; it can perform no acts of its own" (I.4).

So the living flame of love is the Holy Spirit, and this book could well be called a treatise on the Holy Spirit. *The Spiritual Canticle* reflects on "the Word, the Son of God, hidden in the innermost being of the soul" (I.6); *The Living Flame* treats of "the interior assault of the Holy Spirit, making it divine" (I.35).

Stanza II explains how the three Persons of the most Holy Trinity effect the work of divine union. The "sweet cautery" of the Holy Spirit burns and wounds only to relieve, causing delight; the "pure touch of the divinity"—the gentle hand of the Father, the delicate touch of the Word, infinitely subtle in the innermost being of the soul— communicates strength, wisdom, love—the very beauty, grace, and goodness of God Himself.

Stanza III deals with matters so profound that St. John exclaims "May God be pleased to grant me His favor here!" The soul "has become God by participation in Him and in His attributes: it is like the air within the flame, which is transformed into the flame itself" (III.9)—the Spirit moving the soul as the fire moves the air that is enkindled. It is like the overshadowing of the Blessed Virgin Mary by the Holy Spirit. The soul experiences a deep perception and experience of the grandeurs of the wisdom and excellences of God. The caverns, or faculties, are wonderfully infused with the splendors of the "lamps of fire", the attributes of God. It actually participates in these attributes of God; it sees that God really belongs to it by "hereditary possession, with the right of ownership, as an adopted child of God."

Stanza IV expresses the soul's deep love of and gratitude to the Beloved for His divine awakening within it, for His secret indwelling, for His sweet breathing within it in gentleness and love: "like the breathing of one awakening from sleep." The Word moves in the depths of the soul's being, it delights in knowing creatures through God, and God through creatures. It is "as though a palace were thrown open": "the veils are drawn aside, God reveals His true nature, the beauty of His being, the beauty of His face, so gracious . . . an experience quite indescribable."

A word should be said on the notable "digressions" of the Saint: I.19–25; II.24–30; III.27–67. All refer to the period of purification disposing the soul for union, and indicate a real preoccupation of the Saint with its importance for the guidance of the soul. It is curious that although the teaching repeats and emphasizes that of *The Dark Night*, the word "night" is not used; nor is there any reference to the night of the senses. Best known of the digressions is III.27–67, in itself a precious "lift-out" on spiritual direction. His message to directors: Remember, the real director, or guide, is the Holy Spirit. Let them not forget it.

Pope John Paul II said of the writings of St. John of the Cross: "I think that to understand the dignity . . . the possibilities of the human person, it is necessary to study, at least once, the theology of St. John of the Cross; study, I mean, the dimension of man [the human person] revealed in his doctrine . . . Then one can never forget his dignity."

While reading *The Living Flame*, we reflect on God's infinite condescension and on the dignity of the human person—on ourselves, on our capacity to be filled with the fullness of God. St. Paul exclaimed long ago: "Eye has not seen, nor ear heard, neither has it entered into the mind of man to conceive the things God has prepared for those who love Him".

John Venard OCD

ABOUT THIS BOOK

The Saint's commentary on each stanza of the poem is on the left-hand pages of this book; on the right-hand page are notes, clarifications, and cross references—especially from St. Teresa and other works of St. John—for those who need some help in reading the text. The purpose of the book is to encourage the reader to proceed to reflective reading of the full text.

Some readers may have difficulty with the use of the word "soul" throughout. Of course, what is meant is "person, the whole person, self", but the Saint used "soul" and substitution of "person" is awkward and unsatisfactory. The translation of the poem aims at accuracy of meaning without loss of the poetic, rhythmic flow of the original. This rhythm, entirely original and innovative in Spanish poetry, reflects the Saint's genius for poetic expression of the ineffable—the gentleness and serenity of God's action inspiring impassioned exclamations of wonder.

We remain conscious of the Saint's reluctance in undertaking this work, and make it our own: "The unwillingness I feel . . . stems from the fact that these matters are so interior and spiritual that words fail to describe them, such is the sublimity of the subject. We must rely on divine Scripture and the better judgement and understanding of the Church, our Mother."

ABBREVIATIONS

Asc.   *The Ascent of Mount Carmel*
D.N.   *The Dark Night of the Soul*
S.C.   *The Spiritual Canticle*
L.F.   *The Living Flame of Love*
W.P.   *The Way of Perfection*
I.C.   *The Interior Castle*

THE LIVING FLAME OF LOVE

Exposition of the stanzas which treat of the most intimate and perfect union and transformation of the soul in God, written by John of the Cross, Discalced Carmelite, at the request of Doña Ana de Penalosa, composed in prayer about the year 1584.

PROLOGUE

The unwillingness I feel in expounding these four stanzas stems from the fact that we are dealing with matters so interior and spiritual that words fail to describe them, such is the sublimity of the subject. We must rely on Divine Scripture and the better judgement and understanding of the Church, our Mother.

It is not to be wondered at that God should give such high and rare favors to those on whom He chooses to bestow them. He is God, and as God He gives with infinite love and tenderness.

These stanzas treat of a love even more perfect than that described in *The Spiritual Canticle*. The log of wood, when placed in the fire, glows more and more as the fire becomes hotter and it becomes one single living flame with it.

The soul, inflamed with divine love, speaks in the following stanzas:

The Poem

O living flame of love
how tenderly you wound
the deepest center of my soul!
Since now no more you afflict me,
bring all, if you will, to a happy ending;
break the web of this sweet encounter.

O sweet cautery!
O delectable wound!
O gentle hand! O delicate touch!
that tastes of eternal life,
and pays every debt!
In killing you have changed death to life.

O lamps of fire!
in whose splendors
the deep caverns of feeling,
which were once obscure and blind,
with exquisite loveliness
give forth both warmth and light to their Beloved!

How gently and lovingly
you awaken in my breast
where secretly, alone, you dwell;
and in your sweet breathing
filled with good and glory
how delicately you make me fall in love!

6

STANZA I

O living flame of love
how tenderly you wound
the deepest center of my soul!
Since now no more you afflict me,
bring all, if you will, to a happy ending;
break the web of this sweet encounter.

Commentary

1. The soul seems now at last
    wholly inflamed in divine union,
    as though rivers of glory, "fountains of living water" (Jn. 7:38),
    flowed from its innermost being.
    Only a slender web, or veil,
    separates it from heavenly joys.
    It addresses the Holy Spirit ("the flame"),
    begging Him to end its mortal life
    in order to arrive at complete and perfect glory;
    so it says, "O living flame of love . . .!"

2. "O" signifies the soul's exultation
    in discovering its new freedom in love,
    along with deep yearning and earnest desire,
    entreating love to set it free.

3. This flame of love is the Holy Spirit,
    dwelling within, consuming, transforming in love—
    a flame which flashes forth in most-precious acts of love.
    These acts are so precious as to be of greater merit and value
    than anything the soul has ever done.
    The acts resemble the flame that flashes forth
    from a log of wood, already enkindled.

4. Just as the angel ascended in the flame
    of the sacrifice of Manoah (Jg. 13:20)
    so, absorbed in this flame—the Holy Spirit—
    the soul's vehement acts of love, no longer its own,
    but those of the Spirit of God,
    rise upward, born aloft to God.
    All its acts are now divine,
    so that whenever this flame breaks forth,
    it seems to enjoy eternal life,
    since all its activity is of God, in God.

1.   The same "flame" which purified the soul in *The Dark Night*
        now transforms it. It is the Holy Spirit—"a flame that consumes
        and gives no pain" (S.C. 39.14). The soul begins to experience
        the unutterable joy of being "wholly inflamed", or kindled with
        love of God. Both St. John of the Cross and St. Teresa wrote
        poems on the theme "Dying because I cannot die." Cf. S.C.
        14, 15.9: "The divine onslaught is like the overwhelming force
        of a river in flood, engulfing the soul". Cf. Jn. 4:14: "The water
        that I shall give will turn into a spring inside him, welling up
        to eternal life."

2.   "O" at the first three verses and "How" at the fourth have a
        special force. These words try to convey the ineffable, or the
        unspeakable depth of the soul's exultant joy, as well as
        expressing the yearning to be set free for God alone.

3.   In *The Dark Night*, the log of wood (the soul) had to be cleansed
        of all its impurities before the living flame could enter into
        it to change it into itself, transforming it. This purification was
        "the dark night." Now the transformation is complete: the log
        is all fire, and the flame, the Holy Spirit, bursts forth; all the
        soul's acts of love are those of the Spirit of God, who is love
        itself. No virtuous or meritorious action in the past is comparable
        in effect to these acts of love performed now by the gift of
        the power of the Spirit.

4.   The text states: "It [the soul] can perform no acts, because
        the Holy Spirit makes them all and moves it towards Him."
        Heaven has already begun—but it is still a foreshadowing of
        the fullness of eternal life, as St. John is at pains to point out
        in paragraph 6 below. Cf. L.F. II.32: the "two kinds of life"—
        (a) beatific, after death; (b) possession of God, in love, in
        this life, that of the "perfect" (of which he is speaking here).
        Cf. also L.F. I.14.

9

5.   This is God's language
for those who are purified, cleansed, aflame with love;
His words are "spirit and life" (Jn. 6:64).
To others, this language may seem distasteful,
as to those who turned away, and walked no more with Him,
when He preached the sweet and loving doctrine of the
Eucharist.

6.   Those who do not relish the language of God
should not think that others do not.
St. Peter and the Samaritan woman
tasted the sweetness of the words of Jesus.
Since the Father, the Son, and the Holy Spirit
are communicated to the soul,
which is transformed into a living flame of love,
why should it be difficult to believe
that it enjoys a foretaste of eternal life?
Although this is not the perfection of eternal life,
it is such a vivid experience of God, so delightful,
that it may be called a taste of the living God,
a glimpse of eternal life, God's life.

7.   *"that tenderly wounds my soul"*:

The soul is wounded with the tenderness of God's life,
like the bride in the Song of Songs:
"as soon as He spoke my soul melted" (5:6).

8.   It is of the nature of love to wound,
but so delicately as to cause love and delight.
The living flame of tender love
touches the soul, again and again, in its innermost depths,
and this even though at any moment
it could be said to be "wholly" consumed in love.
Ravishing are the joy and delight:
"My delight is to be with the children of men" (Prov. 8:30–31).

5.   Compare S.C. Prologue 1: "If these things are not read with the simplicity of the spirit of knowledge and love they contain, they will seem to be absurd, not reasonable." Note the change in metaphor: the interior workings of the Holy Spirit in the purified soul are "the language of God; not perceived by those who have a taste for other things."

6.   St. Peter: "You have the words of eternal life" (Jn. 6:69). The Samaritan woman "forgot the water and the pitcher because of the sweetness of Jesus' words" (*text*). St. John's logic is, Why should we be surprised at anything God does? "There is no reason for marvelling that God should give such rare favors" (L.F., Prologue). Cf. also L.F. II.5: "It is not to be marvelled at that God should bring some souls to so high a state." In S.C. 39.4, we read: "It is not incredible that [we] should understand, know, and love in the Trinity . . . as does the Trinity itself! . . . It is for this that God created us in His image and likeness."

7.   The infinite tenderness of God assuages the wounding; the soul "dissolves in love" (*text*). Cf. Asc. and D.N.: God is likened to (a) a kindly mother and (b) a doctor gently prescribing healing medicine.

8.   The mystery and paradox of God's love: the soul is "totally" cauterized, consumed with love, yet with each divine "touch" the "fullness" becomes more complete. The Blessed Virgin at each moment was "full of grace" yet the divine life ever increased within her. The "fullness" of the Beatific Vision will, of its nature, be forever increasing, eternally.

9.   *"the deepest center"*:

This feast of the Holy Spirit
takes place in the substance of the soul,
whether neither the devil, nor the world,
nor sense can enter.
God, because of the soul's great purity,
communicates himself frequently, abundantly, generously.
The soul simply receives.
This is its only occupation—
to will, and consent gladly to God's action;
all its movements become divine.
There are other centers in the soul,
less profound than the "deepest center" we speak of here.

10.   In speaking of other "centers" of the soul,
we must exclude all notions of space, or parts.
There is no inward or outward, no length or depth;
the intensity illumines all equally.

11.   By the "deepest center" is meant
the limit of an object's power and force of operation
in accordance with its nature.
Fire or rock have a natural point of limitation
which they will attain but cannot pass beyond.
A rock is drawn by its natural power and inclination
to its deepest center by the force of gravity.
If it should arrive at the center of the earth,
it would be at rest—in its "deepest center".

12.   The soul's center is God.
When, with all the strength and power of its being,
it will have reached the limit point,
its final and deepest center in God,
it will know, love, and enjoy God with all its might.
Until it has reached that point,
it can still advance, and is not satisfied.
At any point it can be said to be in its center,
but not in its deepest center.

9.   The substance of the soul: St. Teresa says "in the most innermost
        mansion, where the King dwells", St. John uses the scholastic
        term "substance" but not in its metaphysical sense, i.e. of
        substance supporting accidents. He means the innermost
        depths—the "apex of the soul", the "ground of our being".
        Mystics have tried in vain to put this into words. The soul
        receives; it cooperates in receiving. In *The Spiritual Canticle*
        "its sole occupation is love", in its "deepest center". St. Teresa
        tells us that the happiness we should pray for is to enjoy the
        complete security of the blessed.

10.   We are now being made aware that St. John of the Cross is
        speaking of the "deepest center" in describing the ultimate
        experience possible by God's action. There are degrees of
        "entering within"—degrees of perfection—according to the
        soul's disposition and capacity to receive.

11.   St. John's conclusion that a rock would be at rest in the earth's
        center was later proved—by the discovery of gravity—
        Metaphorically it may be concluded equally that the soul is
        ultimately at rest in God. Paragraph 12 below clarifies this.

12.   This clarifies paragraphs 9–11 above: God is the soul's center;
        also, it is not possible to reach this "deepest center" (in "the
        substance of the soul") in this life. "To know and love God
        in this life and to enjoy Him forever in the next" answers the
        Catechism question "Why did God make you?" To "love God
        with all our might" is the First Commandment.

13.   Love is the power and force which unites us with God.
        The more degrees of love, the more deeply
        we enter into God and center ourselves on Him.
        Each degree is a "center".
        "There are many mansions in my Father's house" (Jn. 14:2).
        So one degree of love would suffice
        to place the soul in its center, God.
        The more degrees of love, the closer the union;
        until God's love wounds it in its deepest center,
        so transforming it that it appears to be God.
        Light shining on crystal so transforms it
        that the crystal seems to be all light;
        the stronger the light, the brighter it seems.

14.   The words "wounded in its deepest center"
        indicate the richness and abundance of delight of the soul
        in receiving the communication of the Holy Spirit,
        which wounds and assails it in its innermost being.
        Not that this wounding is as radical and complete
        as in the beatific vision of the life to come
        (though this may be experienced fleetingly in this life).
        It is possible that the habit, or disposition, of charity
        may be perfectly given by the Holy Spirit in this life,
        but the operation and realization, or fruition,
        always fall short of the perfection of the beatific
        vision, while resembling it.

15.   Since few have had experience of what we are describing,
        it is not surprising that some sceptical people
        will dismiss it as unreal or exaggerated.
        I reply to this that God, who is the "Father of lights"
        takes His delight in being with the children of men.
        Why should it be incredible
        that the promise of the Son of God should be fulfilled—
        that the Blessed Trinity will come to abide with those
        who love Him? (Jn. 14:23).
        By this indwelling
        the intellect is illumined with the Son's own wisdom,
        the will finds its delight in the Holy Spirit,
        and it is powerfully caught up
        in the delightful embrace of the Father.

13.   The importance of any small degree of love is emphasized, echoing St. Teresa's thought in *The Interior Castle*, Mans. I.1: it is a grace in itself to be in the First Mansion—the time of repentance, self-knowledge, turning to God. We are "on the road to divine intimacy." Later, in paragraph 34 below, the Saint will stress the importance of making acts of love, "so that . . . we may not stay long, either in this world or the next, without seeing God." The crystal appears to be all light, but remains itself. But what is crystal in darkness?

14.   St. John uses the scholastic terms "habit" and "operation." God gives the "virtue", the power or fixed disposition, to love Him alone. This is the "habit" of the virtue. In daily living, we exercize the virtue in act—in being charitable, loving God, caring for others. This is the "operation"—the virtue of charity "at work." A trained musician has the "habit"—the capacity, power, and skill to play the instrument; it is not always "in operation."

15.   St. John's reasoning here is as in the Prologue: "He is God, and as God He gives with infinite love and tenderness" (cf. also L.F. II.5). Only those who have experienced what is being described can really grasp the full import of scriptural passages like John 14:23 or, for that matter, any passage of scripture. We recall the words of Origen: "Only those who have rested on the breast of Jesus, with John, will understand his 'mystical' Gospel." Speaking from the depths of his own mystical experience, St. John of the Cross finds it surprising that anyone could be incredulous. "If only you knew the gift of God" (Jn. 4:10). Cf. also L.F. II.5: "Do not marvel that God brings some souls to this state." Cf. also S.C. 39.4: "It is not incredible . . . that she should . . . know and love in the Trinity . . . as does the Trinity itself!"

16.   This operation of the Holy Spirit
is much greater than that which happens
in the transformation of love alone,
which is like a burning coal.
What we are describing is like a furnace enkindled.
There is a certain degree of union in love
in the Church Militant,
but this is not to be compared
with the perfect union in love
of the Church Triumphant.

17.   So, when the soul says,
"O living flame of love/how tenderly you wound",
it feels that divine love, which brings all blessings
with it, is being communicated to it in a vital way:
divine knowledge in the intellect,
divine love in the will,
rejoicing and delight in the memory—
to each faculty according to its capacity to receive.
So, the soul, purified in its inner being, is now touched by
the very inner being of God Himself,
and the Holy Spirit sweetly absorbs the soul,
in a sharing of divine wisdom.

18.   *"Since now no more you afflict me"*:

that is, you do not weary and afflict
as you formerly did.
The flame, which is God, is now gentle and friendly—
not as before, when in the state of purgation,
and the soul was entering upon contemplation.
At this point, we pause to explain this.

16.   We have seen that any degree of love causes a certain transformation in the soul; St. John is emphasizing the very special and wonderful gift of God—which is more like a furnace enkindled than a burning coal. "The soul in which this habitually comes to pass will not be backward in receiving these favors from God" (*text*).

17.   The Saint recapitulates, returning to "O living flame . . ." to emphasize the radical nature of the transformation in God— "touching" not only the faculties, or powers, of the soul (intellect, memory, will) but the very "substance" or being of the soul. All this is brought about by the action of the Holy Spirit; the living flame flares up with its "glorious vibrations" to communicate Divine wisdom. St. John quotes the Book of Wisdom 7:24: "Wisdom is quicker than any motion; she is so pure, she pervades and permeates all things."

18.   This short paragraph makes two important points: (1) the living flame is God, the Holy Spirit; (2) contemplation begins with "entering into" the spiritual purgation, or purification, of the dark night of the spirit. St. John now devotes seven paragraphs (19–25) to summarizing his teaching, as in *The Dark Night*, of the passive night of the spirit. See paragraph 25 below: ". . . all this is treated in *The Dark Night*. This is the first of the Saint's three "digressions" from his main theme: I.19–25 (dark night); II.24–30 (trials of contemplatives); III.27–67 ('anointings', prayer).

19.   The soul is prepared for divine union
        by the work of the Holy Spirit, the flame—
        purifying and cleansing its evil habits and imperfections.
        The fire of love which is united to
        the soul in divine union is the fire which purifies
        and cleanses, just as the fire which penetrates a
        log of wood is the same which cleanses it of its
        impurities, preparing it to be transformed into fire.
        This causes great suffering both in the spirit and the senses.
        The flame, far from being sweet and gentle,
        causes only darkness in affliction,
        along with keen awareness of the soul's innate weakness.
        Sometimes it experiences love, but with torment;
        sometimes it experiences consolation,
        only to be afflicted still further with bitter trials.
        The worst trial is that of increasing self-knowledge,
        a spiritual trial which an be unutterably painful.

20.   The soul is afflicted with darkness in the intellect,
        great aridity in the will,
        and, in the memory, acute awareness of its misery
        as it becomes more delicately sensitive in self-knowledge.
        In the depths of its being, its sense is of abandonment.
        There is no consolation in anything,
        and it cannot even raise its heart to God,
        so oppressive is the purifying flame.
        God seems to be cruel and heartless.

21.   The suffering at this time cannot be put into words;
        it seems to be little less than that of purgatory.
        This state is best described by Jeremiah
        in the Book of Lamentations 3.1-9.
        As Tobias laid his heart on the coals
        so that every kind of evil spirit might be driven out,
        so the soul must submit to remedies and cures
        as prescribed by God to bring it health.

18

19.   For the comparison of the log of wood being transformed in the fire, compare D.N. II.10. The aptness of the comparison at once becomes evident; the same fire prepares the wood— cleansing it of impurities, drying it, bringing it to the required degree of heat, disposing it to be inflamed—and changes it into fire, so that it becomes one with it. Applying this to the purifying of the soul (log of wood) by the Holy Spirit (flame), St. John goes on to say that "spiritual persons call this the purgative way." This is confusing. What he is describing is obviously the suffering, or darkness, of the passive night of the spirit. This is, according to his own words in "The Theme" of *The Spiritual Canticle*, the illuminative way—that of proficients, not of beginners (the purgative way). Is the Saint mistaken here or does he think of the purgative way, as used here, as the purification of both senses and spirit—together? The question remains.

20.   The real cause of suffering is a heightened sense of one's own misery before God: self-knowledge: "Its spiritual eye gives it a clear knowledge of itself" (*text*). This leads to a sense of being abandoned by God—as though God must of necessity leave one so unworthy to his own devices. Prayer becomes distasteful, seemingly impossible. St. Teresa says: "God gives a lively knowledge of Himself, with keen distress because of His absence" (I.C. Mans. VI.11). Cf. S.C. 13 *et seq.*

21.   St. John frequently describes the passive night of the spirit by likening it to the pains of purgatory; see D.N. and paragraph 24 below. Similarly St. Teresa: "a suffering which resembles that of purgatory" (I.C. Mans. VI.11). The long passage attributed by St. John to Jeremiah, and to be found in the liturgy to the Lord's Passion, seems to the Saint to be an exact description of the dark night of the spirit. One could wish that he had continued the quotation from the Book of Lamentations: 3, 19–26—with its message of consolation and hope.

22.   Just as the impurities and moisture in the log
       become apparent only when it is exposed to the fire,
       so the soul becomes aware of its impurity and imperfection
       only when assailed by the divine living flame,
       which afflicts and causes pain.
       When it is purified, it can recognize the action of God.
       At first its spiritual eye is darkened
       in the brightness of God.
       Light and darkness, being contraries, cannot coexist.

23.   This divine flame is loving and tender,
       and as the soul becomes increasingly conscious
       of the gentleness and tenderness of God,
       it becomes deeply aware of its own hardness and aridity
       and of how sinful and disordered in its affections
       it really is.
       This awareness of its poverty, sinfulness, and misery
       is heightened by the sense of God's goodness.
       But God continues to perfect and transform,
       so that poverty becomes wealth,
       and misery gives way to joy.

24.   Few people experience this severe purgation,
       which varies in intensity
       according to the Lord's desire to raise the soul
       to a higher degree of union with Him,
       and according to the soul's impurity and imperfection.
       So the purifying pain resembles that of purgatory,
       where souls suffer in order to be purified for the vision of God.
       Through this passive purification of the spirit,
       we can be transformed in God in this life, through love.

25.   As to the intensity of this purification,
       and its effect on intellect, memory, and will,
       and the substance of the soul,
       its various stages and how they are recognized—
       all this is treated in the Dark Night of the Soul.
       It suffices to recall here
       that God Himself purifies the soul,
       in order to transform it.

22.   Again, the log of wood. We are blissfully unaware of much
       imperfection and sinfulness, even when some progress has been
       made in the early stages of the spiritual life. Some, while only
       "beginners", think that they have "arrived." St. John deals with
       imperfections of beginners in the first book of the *Dark Night*.
       The discovery of one's deep-seated spiritual poverty and
       sinfulness, in the light of God's action in the passive night
       of the spirit, is indeed painful. The flame seems to afflict, to
       cause pain, until the light of God, at first not recognized because
       the "spiritual eye" is blinded by the divine light, gradually dispels
       the darkness, transforming and illumining the soul. In *The
       Ascent*, St. John speaks of the soul as being blinded by the
       noonday sun.

23.   St. John continues the theme of the impossibility of coexistence
       of opposites: first, darkness and light; now, on the one hand
       God's infinite tenderness, on the other the soul's own hardness
       and its reluctance to give up unlawful affections and attachments
       which remain to hinder the fullness of God's transforming love.
       The pain is in the fact that we thought we were holy; now
       the reality of the situation is all too evident—our sinfulness
       is exposed in the nearness of God. Truth will out. It is painful.
       The Saints all experienced this increasing awareness of
       sinfulness (without actual sin) the closer they came to God.
       It could be reckoned a "mystical" grace.

24.   As in paragraph 21, the night of the spirit is likened to purgatory.
       In this state, also, the soul being "assailed by the living flame
       of God's love" sees suffering in its true light—its necessity,
       its value. Paradoxically it finds joy in suffering. Few are privileged
       to suffer in this way; few have the courage to answer the call
       "Take up your cross and follow me" in its fullest sense. Yet
       St. John also implies that the Lord may not desire that all should
       be raised to the height of love envisaged here.

25.   This paragraph completes the brief excursus on the dark night
       of the spirit. St. John re-emphasizes that all is God's doing:
       we are passive, receptive, disposing ourselves as best we can
       to accept the pain and the joy of being purified, knowing that
       "the flame which afflicts and causes pain will become very
       sweet to it" (*text*).

26.   This is what the soul means by
        "since now no more you afflict me". This means
        "since now you are the divine light of my understanding
        which before was in such darkness,
        you are the strength of my will.
        I can now love and enjoy you,
        intent only on love, while before I was weak and faint.
        In the innermost substance of my soul
        I am free to glory and delight in you,
        whereas formerly all seemed pain and affliction."

27.   *"bring all, if you will, to a happy ending"*:

        The "happy ending" is the beatific vision,
        the perfection and consummation of the spiritual
        marriage, so ardently desired.
        No matter how close the union with God in this life,
        we still lack complete possession of divine sonship.
        We still live in hope, desiring the fullness of glory
        attainable only in the next life.

28.   The soul is now incapable of pain.
        It wills and desires only what God wills and desires,
        and longs for conformity of sense and spirit.
        In its new and delightful communication with the Spouse
        it recognizes clearly
        the touch and action of the Holy Spirit,
        giving it glimpses of love and glory.
        It feels impelled and invited by the Spirit of God,
        even as the bride in the Song of Songs (S.S. 2:10–14).
        The flame of the Holy Spirit is now tender and sweet,
        so the soul entreats it:
        "Bring all, if you will, to a happy consummation",
        or, as in the Pater Noster,
        "Thy Kingdom come; Thy will be done."
        And that this may come to pass:

26. A turning point—the divine flame no longer causes pain, affliction. We have emerged from the darkness. There is a new sense of glorious freedom—the "freedom of the children of God"—enlightenment in understanding, a new strength in love, a deep inner peace, and joy in the certainty of loving and being loved. Suffering does not cease; the cross is always there. But our attitude to suffering has changed. By the strengthening grace of the Holy Spirit we can find joy in suffering, as the Apostles, transformed by the Spirit, rejoiced to be scourged and to suffer for Christ.

27. There is a difficulty of translation here: literally, "Bring to an end, or complete, if you will." The Saint adds, explaining: "That is to say, perfect the consummation of the spiritual marriage with your beatific vision." He re-emphasizes: wonderful as the spiritual marriage is in this life, it is not yet the perfect union of "consummation" in the beatific vision.

28. This does not mean physical pain. The pain of the dark night of the spirit is spiritual suffering: apparent absence of God, seeming abandonment by God, uncertainties and anxieties about one's spiritual state, aridities in prayer. The soul now rises above these afflictions. They do not necessarily cease, but they no longer afflict so severely. Suffering is now seen in perspective (this explains why the Saints can talk about "joy in suffering", "rejoicing in trials"). This is certainty in God's presence: "She feels this divine companionship within herself" (I.C. Mans. VII.1). Certainty, too, of the Holy Spirit's action—always sanctifying, renewing, beckoning to greater heights of love, tenderly, sweetly—this is the Kingdom—God's will is being done. This accords exactly with St. Teresa's equating of the "Kingdom" with contemplation (W.P. XXX–XXX11).

29.   *"break the web of this sweet encounter"*:

It is easy to reach God
once the obstacles to union are removed—
once the "webs are broken."
The obstacles, or "webs" are three:
temporal, or created things;
natural, our natural desires and inclinations;
sensual, the union of soul and body.
During the purification of the spirit,
when the flame was severe, causing affliction,
the first two "webs" were broken.
The third web, that of the union of soul and body,
is still to be broken,
but this time gently, sweetly, delectably—
the more so as it seems to the soul
that it is to be released from this mortal life.

30.   Although these souls pass through death like others,
the cause and manner of their death is very different.
Even though they should die from infirmity or old age,
their spirits are wrested away
by a profound, sublime, loving impulse.
The web is broken; that jewel—their spirit—is borne away.
Their death is thus gentle, like that of the swan,
which sings most gently and sweetly
just before it dies.

31.   When, therefore, God permits the soul to see itself
enriched with virtues,
and in perfect and complete possession of the Kingdom,
and this without the slightest trace of presumption,
it is so consumed with desire
to break the frail web of this natural life
and to see itself with Christ
that it begs, "Break the web of this sweet encounter."

29. Now the "encounter" with the flame is sweet and delightful (formerly the soul was "assailed" in its breaking off of attachments to created things and its own natural appetites). Now the Spirit, the living flame, purifies gently, and there is sweetness in the anticipation of the web of life being broken: "We know . . . we have a dwelling place of God in the heavens" (2 Cor. 5:1).

30. "Precious in the eyes of the Lord is the death of His Saints" (Ps. 115:15). St. John comments: "The rivers of love of the soul are about to enter the sea." It is not surprising that the death of the Saints seems to be just a gentle "passing-over." In St. Paul's terms, the victory over death has been won many times over in the life of the baptized, virtuously and nobly lived. We have only to recall the Saints' deaths—John of the Cross, Teresa, Thérèse, Francis. St. Teresa of Avila on her deathbed: "It is time that my soul should rest in you whom I have so much desired."

31. Humility lies in the truth of accepting gratefully whatever God has done in us. "He has done great things for me" ("Magnificat"). Along with the realization of possessing all the virtues is the certainty that all is God's doing. Presumption or pride is impossible; only joyous thanksgiving and an all-consuming desire "to be dissolved, and be with Christ."

32.   Even as a web is so transparent
        that light can shine through it,
        so the bond between flesh and spirit
        which separates God and the soul
        is so refined and spiritualized
        that divinity can shine through it.
        The soul becomes increasingly conscious
        of the power of the life to come
        and in doing so feels keenly the weakness of this life
        which seems as fragile as a very fine spider's web.
        It sees everything with the eyes of God,
        having entered the consciousness of God,
        to whom "a thousand years are as yesterday",
        and all things and all nations are as nothing.

33.   The soul asks that the web be "broken"
        rather than "cut" or "allowed to wear out",
        because an encounter is more properly broken—
        rather than cut, or worn out.
        The strong, forceful contacts of love
        are caused by the breaking of the web;
        as love acts quickly, briefly, vehemently,
        so spiritual acts of love, infused by God,
        are performed in the soul in an instant,
        and with great intensity,
        since the soul is thoroughly disposed to receive them.
        Again, "broken" is apt
        as the soul desires the web of life
        to be quietly destroyed.

34.   The soul which is really in love with God
        desires and begs that its life might be ended
        by a sudden assault of love,
        knowing that God takes to Himself before their time
        those souls whom He specially loves:
        "Being made perfect in a short space,
        they fulfill a long time."
        It is important to practice acts of love in this life,
        so that, made perfect in a short time,
        we may not stay long, either in this world or the next,
        without seeing God.

32.   The senses no longer dominate; the spirit is in control. The
       soul is "spiritualized", refined, transparent. This life—so short,
       so fragile—is now seen in the perspective of God, in the light
       of eternity. See S.C. 37.2: "[The soul] will know the sublime
       mysteries of God and man" as well as union with divine wisdom.
       The soul has "entered the consciousness of God."

33.   The Saint lists four reasons why the term "break the web" is
       more apt. The reasons given are somewhat obscure, as is the
       whole paragraph. In this state of perfection there is no longer
       need of successive acts over a period of time, in a protracted
       effort to dispose oneself for God's action; this is now assured.
       Love acts swiftly, with vehemence, and brief acts of love are
       now more efficacious than the painful, protracted efforts of
       the early stages. "The short prayer pierces the heavens" when
       it is inspired by great love. St. Thérèse tells us she needed
       only one short prayer from the Song of Songs: "Draw me, we
       will run after you to the odor of your ointments" ("we" includes
       all who needed her intercessory prayer at that time).

34.   The text quoted is from Wisdom 4:10-11, 13-14. The difficulty
       about St. John's reasoning in this and other passages in this
       action is that, as is obvious from experience, God does not
       always take all good and holy people to Himself before their
       time. Some of the Saints lived to a ripe old age! Nevertheless
       the text—"for his soul was pleasing to God, therefore He
       hastened to take him out of this life"—may be considered
       generally true. Note well the Saint's implication as he notes
       the importance of acts of love.

35.   These interior assaults of the Holy Spirit
        are called encounters
        because the soul is conscious of an infinite desire
        that its life may come to an end.
        This not yet being accomplished,
        God assaults it—encounters it—to purify it,
        penetrating to the core of its being,
        deifying it, making it divine.
        The Being of God absorbs the soul beyond all being.
        This assault is a piercing of the Holy Spirit
        eminently sweeter than anything yet experienced.

36.   Summing up Stanza I: The soul says,
        "O flame of the Holy Spirit, that pierces my soul
        so intimately and tenderly, cauterizing it—
        since I am purified and greatly strengthened,
        my petitions are so much more effective than before,
        and I now ask only what you desire me to ask.
        You desire to give yourself to me eternally,
        so, praying with delight and rejoicing in you,
        I beg you to break the slender web of this life.
        Not that old age will cut it in a natural way,
        but that I may be able to love you
        with the fullness and satisfaction I so much desire,
        and this forever and ever."

35.   In *The Spiritual Canticle*, as here, St. John speaks of the "divine onslaught" which is "like the overwhelming force of a river in flood" (S.C. 14, 15.9). The Holy Spirit now takes possession of the soul—"the spiritual, interior voice similar to that of the Holy Spirit coming to the Apostles like a mighty wind" (S.C. 14, 15.10). Yet "being is absorbed in Divine Being with a sweetness eminently sweeter than all other encounters" (*text*). Strength, power, allied to gentleness: this is characteristic of the Spirit's action in "deifying" the soul.

36.   In Stanza II of *The Spiritual Canticle*, commenting on "May the vision of your beauty be my death", St. John says, "The soul does not show outstanding virtue in wanting to die . . . To desire death is in itself a natural imperfection." In the early stages of the spiritual life, the desire for death (not uncommon) may be just a form of escapism! Now, however, the longing for death is from the Holy Spirit. Whereas, before, "impatient love did not allow me to be so conformed to the conditions of this life in which you desired me still to live" (*text*), now only one thing matters: in every moment, the will of God. This very conformity to the will of God empowers us to ask that life may end, a petition made at the instance of the Holy Spirit: ". . . my judgement now issuing from your countenance" (Ps. 16:2).

STANZA II

O sweet cautery!
O delectable wound!
O gentle hand! O delicate touch!
that tastes of eternal life
and pays every debt!
In killing you have changed death into life.

Commentary

1.   In this stanza the soul explains
how the three Divine Persons of the Most Holy Trinity
effect this work of divine union,
though the whole work is attributed to only one: "You."
The "sweet cautery", a "delectable wound", is the Holy Spirit.
The "delicate touch"—the desire for eternal life—is the Son.
The "gentle hand", transforming the soul, is the Father.

2.   *"O sweet cautery!"*:

This signifies the Holy Spirit, a consuming fire
which transforms into itself the soul that it touches,
burning and cauterizing according to the soul's disposition.
This infinite fire of love burns with such vehemence
and intensity that the soul not only feels the burn
but seems to become a cautery of blazing fire.

3.   It is wonderful that the soul is not consumed
in this vehement fire, which could consume a thousand worlds.
Neither does it cause affliction,
but brings it delight, deifying it,
glowing and burning in it gently.
This is due to the purity and perfection
with which the spirit burns in the Holy Spirit.
In this way the Spirit descended on the disciples
gathered in the upper room at Pentecost.
It came on them with vehemence,
and they burned inwardly and sweetly in love.
This fire does not afflict, or weary the soul,
but rather enlarges and delights it.

1.   Every action of God is the work of all three Divine Persons,
      but theologians make no difficulty about attributing special
      works to one or other of the Persons. Power, wisdom, knowledge,
      and other attributes are sometimes "appropriated" to the Divine
      Persons—e.g. power to the Father, wisdom to the Son, goodness
      to the Holy Spirit. We may say that the Father creates, the Son
      redeems, and the Holy Spirit sanctifies. Yet all that God does
      proceeds from the undivided will of the undivided Trinity. St.
      John feels at liberty to attribute, or appropriate, specific works
      to each Divine Person. Cf. St. Teresa, *Spiritual Relations* V:
      ". . . though in some strange way the Persons are apprehended
      by soul as distinct, it realizes that they are one God." See also
      Spiritual Relations XXXIII.

2.   The Holy Spirit's action is at once delightful and not painful:
      "God is pleased to touch the soul with some vehemence" (*text*).
      Cauterization, which is burning, wounds, and causes pain, but
      the wound heals. This burning is without pain or affliction.
      The soul is conscious only of the sweetness of the cauterization,
      being caught up and entirely transformed into the Holy Spirit.

3.   The Holy Spirit, descending on the disciples at Pentecost,
      transformed them—the tongues of fire symbolized the interior
      change. Henceforth they burned with zeal for the Kingdom
      (before they were cautious and lacked courage). The same
      Holy Spirit still descends on those purified to receive His
      action—to transform, even to deify them. His action is at once
      gentle and vehement, causing delight, not affliction or pain.

4.   So the soul that happily receives this cautery
        knows all things, tastes all things,
        does all that it desires, and prospers.
        No one prevails against it, nothing touches it.
        "The spiritual man judges all things:
        he himself is judged by no one" (1 Cor. 2:15).
        This is characteristic of love:
        to seek out all the good things of the Beloved.

5.   O you who have merited this supreme fire,
        how great is your glory.
        While it could consume you, annihilate you,
        it does not, but consumes you rather in glory.
        Do not marvel that God brings some souls to this state.
        If the cautery itself is so sweet,
        how delightful it must be to be touched by it!

6.   "O delectable wound!:

        The soul now speaks to the wound.
        It is sweet and delightful,
        since the cautery is a cautery of love.

7.   While a cautery of fire always causes a wound,
        which can be healed only by applying salves,
        this divine cautery of love can be cured
        only by the same burning that caused the wound.
        With each new burning, as it touches the wound,
        it inflicts a greater wound of love—
        curing and healing as it wounds the more—
        until, completely cauterized with successive woundings,
        the soul comes to be wholly dissolved in a wound of love.
        It is thus altogether wounded, but altogether healthy.
        This cautery of love wounds with love
        whether the soul is already perfect
        or wounded with miseries and sins.

4.   "The spiritual man searches all things, even the deep things of God" (1 Cor. 2:10). The soul lives and moves in a new kind of life, at a new level of being. Everything it does is for God, with God, inspired by God. What is merely earthly, of this world, cannot absorb it or affect it. Everything is viewed in the light of God, and is done out of love.

5.   What could consume and annihilate the soul gives glory. What precisely does St. John mean here and elsewhere by "glory"? Strictly speaking, glory belongs to God alone. In the Old Testament it usually means a visible manifestation of the divinity—"holiness manifest." To give glory to Yahweh is to recognize His divinity. Jesus revealed His glory at the Transfiguration. St. Paul holds out to Christians the hope of sharing in God's glory (Rom. 5:2); the Christian, like Christ, will rise to glory (1 Cor. 15:40). At the last Supper, Jesus promised that His disciples will share in His glory, which He will communicate to them (Jn. 17:22, 24). St. John of the Cross speaks of a "consummation in glory" for those touched by the fire of the Holy Spirit. Cf. Jn. 16:12: "When the Spirit of Truth comes He will lead you to the complete truth. . . . He will glorify me."

6.   This wound causes no pain. Cf. S.C.39.14, where St. John comments on ". . . with a flame that consumes and gives no pain." At S.C. 39.14 he describes "a consuming flame that brings to completion or perfection. . . . God consummates and restores."

7.   St. John says that the Holy Spirit acts "like a good physician" who "inflicted the wound only to relieve it." He is at pains to remind us that the Spirit breathes where He wills, and this "cautery" or "burn" can happen to imperfect as well as perfect souls. This might seem to contradict all he has said about predisposition and purification of the soul; but God's action cannot be limited, as sudden and dramatic conversions testify. The paradox: the soul is continually being wounded, but becomes more healthy until "dissolved in a wound of love." St. Paul: "I desire to be dissolved, and be with Christ."

8.   This is the highest degree to which any soul can attain,
        since it touches the substance of the soul
        and is therefore the more sublimely delectable.
        It is a pure touch of divinity, without form or figure,
        neither intellectual nor imaginary.
        God may cauterize the soul in many other ways,
        but none so sublime as this.

9.   The soul may also be cauterized in a sublime way
        which is experienced in the intellect.
        When the soul is enkindled with love of God
        it will experience an assault upon it
        made by a seraph with an arrow or dart
        which will pierce the soul in its very substance.
        It becomes enkindled like a coal, a flame
        which bursts forth suddenly and vehemently
        as happens when a glowing fire is poked in a furnace.
        The pain of wounding causes unspeakable delight,
        the wound being assuaged
        as though by a healing herb.

10.   From this intimate point of the wound—
        which is like a tiny mustard seed—
        the soul sends its enkindling fire
        to all points of its spiritual being.
        Its love becomes refined in this heat
        so that it seems to have within it
        seas of a loving fire
        which reaches to the very limits of earth and heaven.
        The whole universe becomes a sea of endless love
        in which the soul is engulfed,
        so overwhelmed that it can only guess
        at the boundaries of this love.

11.   Now the soul realises how apt is the comparison
        of the Kingdom of Heaven to a tiny mustard seed,
        which grows into a great tree (Matt. 13:31).
        The tiny, enkindled point of love
        blazes out to become a vast furnace of love.

8.   We recall I.9–14 above: "in its deepest center." The Saint says,
      "The soul's center is God" (I.12). It is a "feast of the Holy
      Spirit" (I.9), a pure, sublime touch of God, "neither intellectual
      nor imaginary." It is "a pure touch of divinity" unalloyed, so
      to speak, by intellectual or imaginary experience.

9.   This "transverberation of the heart" happened to St. Teresa in
      1559 and is described in *The Life*, chapter XXIX. It seemed
      to her that an angel, "very beautiful, his face aflame," holding
      in his hand a long golden spear with a tip of red-hot iron,
      pierced her heart, penetrating to her very entrails. This caused
      her excruciating pain (not physical, but spiritual) which,
      however, "caused her greater bliss than any that can come
      from the whole of creation." St. Teresa said that, after this,
      "One's soul could not be content with anything less than God."

10.   In the next paragraph the mustard-seed simile, which St. John
      suddenly introduces here, will be explained. This whole
      paragraph is difficult: St. John is grasping for words and images
      that might "explain the unexplainable"—the experience of being
      a tiny pinpoint in the boundless universe, yet so sparked with
      divinity and inflamed with love that this reaches out to the
      limits of creation, to encompass and impregnate all things with
      love. The soul knows this is happening but cannot clearly
      discern its effects. The soul is beside itself with love.

11.   The mystic interprets the Gospel at a deep level, going beyond
      that required by the ordinary reader. The Church grows from
      the mustard seed—small beginnings—to become a mighty tree
      worldwide. While this is true, more profoundly the soul really
      enkindled with love will radiate its own living love to the whole
      world, to everybody and everything, and beyond—to "worlds
      beyond this world", to infinite horizons. Cf. S.C. 29.2: "For a
      little of this pure love is more precious to God and the soul
      and more beneficial to the Church . . . than all other works
      put together."

12.   Few attain this high state, but some do;
        especially those whose virtue and doctrine
        are destined to be handed on to their children.
        This is because God gives to founders
        both the first fruit of the Spirit, and special gifts
        commensurate with the number of their descendants,
        who are to follow their doctrine and spirituality.

13.   Sometimes the effect of the transverberation,
        or piercing of the soul by a seraph,
        will be felt in the body, which is wounded visibly,
        as happened when St. Francis received the stigmata.
        When this happens, the bodily pain seems all the sweeter
        the greater the degree of love burning in the soul.
        But if it is not manifested outwardly in this way,
        the pleasure and delight in the pain experienced in the soul
        are all the purer and more exquisite.

14.   Those who hope for some supernatural experience
        by means of the senses alone are in error.
        In fact, bodily senses and their operation
        must be set aside.
        However, the spiritual effect may overflow to the senses
        with great spiritual benefit, as in the case of St. Paul.
        So intense was his realization of Christ's sufferings
        that he could say, "I bear in my body
        the marks of the Lord Jesus" (Gal. 6.17).

15.   The soul now turns its attention to
        the hand that inflicts the cautery and to the "touch".
        It praises and extols, not attempting to explain,
        saying, "O gentle hand! O delicate touch!"

12.   This brings into relief a truth about the higher ways of the mystical life which we must always bear in mind. The graces given are graces in the strict meaning of that word—freely given, gratuitous; not given because merited, but given out of God's free choice. Exceptional holiness is usually found in those who have been chosen by God for some special work within the Church—for example, founding an Order.

13.   St. John returns to "the work done by the seraph" in transverberation, or the piercing of the soul with an arrow of divine love. He finds the explanation of the stigmata, or imprinting of the five wounds of Christ on the body, in the fact that it is an expression or manifestation in the body of what takes place in the innermost depths of the soul. We are sufficiently aware of the power of mind over body not to presume always a supernatural source for all such bodily manifestations and St. John would contend (see next paragraph) that the supernatural element always begins in the soul, and may or may not be seen or experienced outwardly in the body.

14.   The Greek word for "marks" is *stigmata*. But *stigmata* does not mean in Greek what it means in English today. St. Paul's sufferings, as described in 2 Cor. 12:7 (illness), Acts 16:22 (beating), 2 Cor. 11:25 (floggings) and Acts 14:19 (stoning) are the "marks", or "brands", that mark him as the "slave of Christ Jesus" (Rom. 1:1, Gal. 1:10). In antiquity *stigmata* was the word used for the branding that marked a slave or an animal as someone's possession. So it is questionable whether "stigmata" as we understand it is what is meant here by St. Paul. St. John wishes to stress the spiritual origin of a genuine stigmata, which is an exteriorization in the senses of an intense spiritual action of God on the soul. Such phenomena can, it seems, be produced in some people by a psycho-pathological process.

15.   So far we have considered only the "sweet cautery", the "delicate wound". The next six paragraphs deal with "the touch of the substance of God in the substance of the soul." There is no attempt at explanation; the Saint reflects on and recalls a precious experience of the Trinity—a touch of God "which savors of eternal life."

16.   This "hand" is the merciful, all-powerful Father—
rich, yet open-handed and generous; touching softly,
graciously—a "gentle hand", even when chastizing.
This "touch" is powerful enough to consume the whole world.
It is none other than the only begotten Son,
the splendor of the Father's glory,
the image of His substance, who is wisdom itself.
"He reaches from end to end, mightily" (Wis. 8:11).

17.   The Word, the Son of God, subtly penetrates
the substance of the soul, absorbing it completely
in the delicacy of His Divine Being,
revealing Himself sweetly and powerfully—
as to Elijah, in the gentle breeze, on Mt Horeb,
not in the power and might of rocks and mountains.
The world can know nothing of this divine gentleness.
It is known only to those
who have withdrawn from worldly things,
refined and purified, and in whom
God dwells secretly, securely, hiding them
in the hiding-place of His presence—the Word.

18.   This touch, so strong and powerful, yet so delicate,
removes the soul
from all other touches of created things
and so draws it to itself in loving union
that all other touches, by comparison, seem coarse and tainted.
All other touches are a grievous torment.

19.   The soul has the capacity
to receive the delicate touch of the Word
because of its remarkable purity and refinement.
And the purer it is,
the more subtly the touch is infused into it..

16.   Here we may recall the first paragraph of this stanza: "The
       soul explains how the three Divine Persons of the Most Holy
       Trinity effect this work of Divine union." The merciful Father
       touches the soul powerfully, gently, generously; but the "touch"
       of the Father is a person—the Divine Person of the Son, given,
       communicated; a continued and continuing gift of "wisdom
       itself." This is "the unction of the Holy Spirit" (L.F. II.22). In
       the text, St. John apostrophizes, or addresses, the hand, the
       touch—and continues in this vein up to and including paragraph
       20.

17.   The Saint emphasizes God's gentleness, delicacy, refinement,
       in His relations with us, especially in this delicate "touch" which
       is the very person of our Lord Jesus Christ, "the Word, the
       Son of God." Elijah, on the mountain, found God not in the
       mighty wind, or the earthquake, the fire, or the tumbling rocks,
       but in the gentle breeze of contemplation. "Touched" by God,
       he cries out, "I am filled with jealous zeal for Yahweh Sabaoth"
       (1 Kings 19:12–14). "Sweetly and powerfully," St. Teresa says,
       "from this companionship [of the Most Holy Trinity] there came
       to the soul a power which had dominion over the whole earth"
       (*Spiritual Relations* XXIV). St. John speculates as to whether
       Elijah receives "substantial knowledge" of God in the
       understanding, or intellect, "wherein consists fruition, which
       is to see God."

18.   Detachment results from God's action. In the earlier stages of
       the spiritual life we are conscious of the need to strive to detach
       ourselves, with God's help, from anything that keeps us from
       God. Now "the soul is so carried out of itself in this trans-
       formation in God that [it] can have attention to no wordly thing.
       . . . [it] shall have the perfect habit of true wisdom" (S.C. 26.14).
       "He makes [the soul] entirely His own, emptying [it] of all [it]
       possesses other than Himself" (S.C. 27.6).

19.   A very difficult paragraph. St. John begins with a generalization:
       "The more delicate a thing is, the broader it is, and the greater
       its capacity; and the more subtle and delicate it is, the more
       diffuse it is, and able to be communicated." His conclusion:
       the greater the soul's purity and refinement, the more subtle,
       delicate, and diffused is the touch of God.

20.   The more subtle and delicate the touch,
        the greater the delight and pleasure it communicates.
        It is ineffable—no words can explain or define it.
        The soul is touched
        with the pure and simple Being of God—
        subtly, lovingly, eminently, delicately.

21.   *"that tastes of eternal life"*:

        Many holy people have experienced this touch of God,
        but none could ever describe it, or explain it.
        It can only be felt, experienced, savored in profound silence.
        We recall
        "the white stone given to him who conquers" (Rev. 2:17);
        no one knows the name thereon
        except the one who receives it.
        In one such single touch, which tastes of eternal life,
        many precious gifts are lavished on the soul:
        fortitude, wisdom, love, beauty, grace, goodness.

22.   Sometimes the unction of the Holy Spirit
        overflows into the body,
        penetrating sweetly and powerfully
        to the very marrow of the bones,
        so that every part of the body
        rejoices in the soul's glory
        and praises God in its own way.
        Since no words can convey the joy of this experience,
        let us simply repeat that it "tastes of eternal life."

23.   *"and pays every debt!"*:

        The "tasting of eternal life" seems ample recompense
        for all the trials endured in arriving at this state.
        In fact, the soul feels excessively rewarded,
        having received the hundredfold promised in the Gospel;
        for every tribulation or trial experienced
        there corresponds a hundredfold of consolation
        in this life. Hence "every debt is paid."

20.   St. John reiterates and briefly summarises. But his last word
        on these "divine touches" is *ineffable*—that is, "not to be spoken
        about—indescribable—unexplainable." They have "neither
        bulk nor weight, mode or manner; they are free from weight,
        form, figure, or accident—anything that restricts or limits
        substance." There is delight in the subtlety of the touch and
        the wonder of being able to discern the movement of God
        in the soul, causing joy and delight in the whole person.

21.   The paradox: the best description of this touch of God is silence.
        The Saint says, "Nor would I willingly speak thereof, lest it
        should be supposed that it is no more than that which I say."
        The only thing that can really be said of it with truth is that
        it "tastes of eternal life." Heaven, in a sense, is brought forward.

22.   St. Teresa says: "It is quite certain that, with the strength it
        has gained, the soul . . . helps the body itself. This strength
        overflows into the weak body".

23.   Another example of the "mystical" interpretation of Scripture.
        A superficial reading of Matthew 19:23 would lead us to the
        conclusion that the Lord is speaking of material reward only
        as the "hundredfold". St. John interprets it also as the more
        than ample recompense for the trials and purification of the
        dark night. He now devotes seven paragraphs (24–30) to
        discussing the trials of contemplatives.

24.   No soul can attain to this sublime state
        without first passing through many tribulations
        and trials.

25.   There are three kinds of trials:
        fears and temptations from mixing with the world;
        aridities and afflictions from the senses;
        darkness and the sense of abandonment in the spirit.
        Just as a precious liquid
        is placed only in a strong container
        which has been prepared by cleansing,
        so this sublime union cannot be enjoyed in this life
        unless the soul has been strengthened
        and prepared by suffering,
        in darkness of both sense and spirit.
        In the life to come, impure spirits must be purified by fire
        in order to be prepared for union with God.
        In this life, souls must undergo that degree of purgation
        which prepares them for union with God, here and now.
        This happens with greater intensity in some than in others,
        depending on the degree of union
        to which God raises them.

26.   Just as virtue is made perfect in weakness (2 Cor. 12:9),
        so God refines the spirit and the senses
        through the patient endurance of trial and suffering.
        Iron can be fashioned by the craftsman
        only by being placed in the fire, and by hammering.

27.   Why are there so few who reach this high state of union?
        It is not that God wishes it to be so—
        He wants all to be perfect.
        But He finds few who have sufficient endurance
        for even small trials and everyday sufferings.
        They take flight, unwilling to suffer the least discomfort.
        God proceeds no further in purifying them.
        He cannot fulfill their desires for higher perfections,
        as they have chosen the broad way of comfort and consolation,
        which if persisted in leads only to perdition.

24.   Paul and Barnabas, encouraging the disciples to persevere in
        faith, remind them that "all have to experience many hardships
        before we enter the Kingdom of God" (Acts 14:22). "In this
        state," St. John says, "the soul suffers no more."

25.   This and the following paragraphs are a résumé of St. John's
        teaching in *The Dark Night.*

26.   Three quotations from Scripture are to be noted: "You have
        sent fire into my bones and have instructed me" (Lam. 1:13);
        "You have chastized me, Lord, and I was instructed" (Jer. 31:18);
        "What can he know who is not tried? And he that has no
        experience knows little" (Sirach 34:9–10).

27.   This paragraph is of special importance; many people ask the
        question. St. John's answer is, Refusal to take up the cross.
        He quotes Matthew 25:21: "Well done, good and faithful servant;
        because you have been faithful in small things, I will trust you
        with greater." He also quotes Jeremiah 12:5: "If you find it
        exhausting to race against men on foot, how will you compete
        against horses?"

        Note: "He cannot fulfill our desires." Desires are all-important
        but they must be accompanied by determination and patient
        endurance. James and John wanted first places in the Kingdom;
        Jesus asked them, "Can you drink the chalice?" St. Teresa says:
        "We should reply, 'We can', for the Lord gives the strength
        to those who have need of it" (I.C. Mans. VI.11).

28.   If souls who desire to walk in security and consolation
        only knew how necessary suffering is,
        they would not seek out comfort
        either from God or creatures.
        Rather they would carry the cross
        and desire to drink the gall and vinegar,
        patiently enduring small exterior trials.
        God would then single them out
        and purify them more profoundly
        through deeper spiritual trials
        in order to give them more interior blessings.
        Those whom God favors with severe interior trials
        must have performed many services for Him
        with admirable patience and constancy.

29.   So God acts with those He desires to exalt.
        He brings them to union with Divine Wisdom,
        trying and testing them as silver is tried by fire.

30.   So it is of the utmost importance
        that the soul should have much patience and constancy
        whether the trials come from within or without,
        whether they are bodily or spiritual.
        They should be accepted as coming from God's healing hand;
        sins, imperfections and evil habits
        are destroyed at the root.
        It is a great favor when God sends these trials,
        and very few deserve
        to be purified and strengthened in this way.

28.   The Saint cites Tobias, of whom Raphael said, "Since you were
        acceptable to God, He favored you by sending you temptation
        that He might try you the more in order to exalt you more"
        (Tb. 12:13). After that trial, the rest of his life was joy. Similarly,
        in the case of Job: "God granted him the favor of sending him
        great trials, that He might afterwards exalt him, both spiritually
        and temporally". St. Teresa writes at length (W.P. Ch. XXXII)
        about our attitude to trials; acceptance depends on love: "I
        believe love is the measure of our ability to bear crosses, great
        or small . . . [trials] are God's gifts in this world . . . those who
        truly love Him will receive love enough to endure them." "The
        soul at last loses its fear of any trials which may befall it"
        (I.C. Mans. VI.11).

29.   "He brings them to union with Divine Wisdom" by which they
        understand and value suffering. Wisdom, which is the gift of
        the Holy Spirit, gives us clear judgment, made in the divine
        light of knowledge of God Himself. We see suffering as God
        sees it—its meaning, its necessity, its value. Cf. S.C. 36. 7–13:
        "Suffering brings with it knowledge of God from within, the
        purest and highest joy" (36.12); "The soul with an authentic
        desire for divine wisdom wants suffering" (36.13).

30.   Patient endurance: it might be said that this is St. John's favorite
        virtue, as it was for St. Paul. Elsewhere he cites St. Paul (2
        Cor. 12:12) recalling "the signs, wonders of his apostleship—
        patient endurance, signs, wonders and mighty deeds." A new
        note is introduced: trials are "a great favor" which "very few
        deserve". Thus ends the "trials" discussion (paragraphs 24–30).

31.   The soul now knows that all is well:
        tribulation gives way to the consolations of the Kingdom.
        For every trial, God gives a corresponding reward,
        repaying with divine gifts for soul and body.
        Hence the words "and pays every debt!"

32.   *"In killing you have changed death to life."*

        Death is privation of life; where there is life,
        there is no death.
        There are two kinds of life:
        the beatific life, the vision of God attained at death;
        and the life of the perfect
        who possess God in union of love,
        which is attained only after complete mortification
        of natural vices and desires.

33.   This is what St. Paul means
        when he speaks of "putting aside the old self"
        in order to "put on the new self
        which is created in God's likeness."
        The "old self" must die completely,
        if this new life is to be lived perfectly.
        In this new life, "the soul's operations become divine."

31.   St. John returns now to the explanation of the words "and pays
       every debt." He is referring to the Book of Esther (4:1–2, 4):
       Mordecai, who wore sackcloth and wept at the gates, refusing
       the fine garment offered by Esther, was finally clothed in royal
       garments and wore a royal crown and the royal ring, symbol
       of kingly power to obtain anything he wanted. St. John says,
       "Those who are in this state obtain everything they want." Every
       debt is paid; their will and the divine will are one; they ask
       only what God desires to give. Cf. S.C. 32.1: "Those who act
       with love and friendship towards God make Him do all they
       desire. The soul that loves holds God a prisoner."

32.   Opposites cannot coexist: love, hatred; light, darkness; life,
       death. Hatred is defined in terms of its opposite, love; it is
       "no-love". Darkness is "no-light". Death is "no-life". There can
       be no life, or union with God, where there is unmortified and
       wilful desire for things that are not of God or which we know
       keep us from God—"our natural vices and desires." These must
       be "completely mortified". The life of the perfect is "possession
       of God", which is life.

33.   The whole passage from Ephesians (4:17–32) should be read
       in the light of St. John's interpretation. St. Paul speaks of "renewal
       in the Spirit" and a "new creation in justice and holiness.
       "Operations" is explained in the following paragraph.

34.   The soul now lives the life of God Himself.
        The intellect no longer depends on the senses for knowledge,
        but knows with a supernatural, divine light.
        It becomes one with the intellect of God.
        The will loves, not in the lowly fashion
        of natural affection, but with divine love,
        moved by the strength of the Holy Spirit.
        God's will and the soul's become one.
        The memory, formerly concerned with created things,
        is so transformed as to have in mind
        only the eternal years.
        The natural desires and affections,
        previously centered only on created things,
        now relish only what is of God.
        In short, all natural movements, operations, inclinations,
        become divine, alive only to God, and the things of God.
        The soul's understanding is that of God;
        its will is that of God; its memory is that of God;
        and its delight is the delights of God.
        The soul is totally under the influence of the Spirit of God.
        The substance of the soul is not the substance of God.
        This could never happen; it remains itself—
        but it has become God by participation in God,
        completely united to and absorbed in Him.
        Nevertheless this union is not as perfect
        as in the next life.

35.   The soul is totally absorbed in divine life,
        withdrawn from all that is of this world.

36.   The soul's state is one of great joy and jubilation;
        aware of its blessedness, its whole life
        becomes a festal song of praise that is always new.
        Its life is wonderfully meritorious in God's sight,
        and there is no need to be amazed
        that every moment is joyful, jubilant praise of God.
        The soul now clearly realizes that God, in His great love,
        wishes ever to lavish on it renewed favors
        and the most intimate, precious, loving words,
        as though it alone existed in His eyes.

34. Perhaps the key sentence in this astonishing paragraph is "The soul, like a true daughter of God, is moved in all things by the Spirit of God." Totally under the influence of the Holy Spirit, the soul is completely open to His action. In another context, St. John says of the Blessed Virgin: "Our Lady, the most glorious Virgin, was raised from the very beginning to this high state of union; she never had the form of any creature impressed on her soul, nor was she moved by any, for she was always moved by the Holy Spirit" (Asc. III . 2, 10). St. John is careful to stress the word "participation". We become "partakers of the divine nature" (2 Pet. 1:2–5), not identified with it (cf. S.C. 39.6). We retain our identity; the "self" is not obliterated. There is complete union, in "differentiated consciousness", to use a modern term. St. John quotes St. Paul: "I live, now not I, but Christ lives in me" (Gal. 2:20); "Death is swallowed up in victory" (1 Cor. 15:54). The Saint quotes Hosea: "O death, I will be your death" (13:14). Cf. S.C. 22 . 3, 4): "The soul thereby becomes divine; becoming God through participation". "The union wrought between the two natures and the communication of the divine to the human is such that even though neither changes its being, both appear to be God." See also S.C. 24.5; 26 . 4, 5, 10.11; 27.7; 31.1; 32.4; 39.4.

35. St. John recalls the Song of Songs: "Although I am black, I am beautiful". All that is natural has been changed into what is divinely beautiful. We have been "brought into the cellars of the King."

36. St. Teresa speaks of "a jubilation and a strange kind of prayer whose nature I cannot ascertain; in this state the soul cannot remain silent, like St. Francis, who could not but praise the Lord aloud" (I.C. Mans. VI.6). The first experience of contemplative prayer, when "their whole desire is hallowing of His Name" (W.P. XXXI), now reaches a climax; every moment is lived out in joyous praise and thanksgiving. One becomes, like Bl. Elizabeth of the Trinity, a "sacrifice of praise." God— loving as only God can, infinitely—loves each soul as though it were the only one in existence. The Saints were very conscious of this; their whole life, like that of the Blessed Virgin Mary, is a renewed "Magnificat": "Death has been changed into life."

51

STANZA III

O lamps of fire!
in whose splendors
the deep caverns of feeling,
once obscure and blind,
with rare splendors
give warmth and light together to their Beloved!

Commentary

1. We need God's help to explain this stanza.
    Those who lack experience may find it wordy, obscure;
    those who have, will probably have no difficulty with it.
    The soul is grateful for the divine knowledge
    God has given it—
    a loving knowledge, communicating light and love,
    which in turn it gives back to the Giver.
    Like any true lover, it is content only in giving its all;
    and the greater the love it gives back,
    the happier it is.
    From the "splendors" of love received,
    it shines brightly in the presence of the spouse,
    giving love for love.

2. Lamps give out both light and heat.
    God, unique and simple in being, *is* His attributes:
    He *is* wisdom, He *is* omnipotence,
    He *is* goodness, He *is* mercy, and all else.
    Each of these attributes is the very being of God,
    Father, Son, and Holy Spirit.
    The soul, being like God, gives forth light and warmth
    through each of God's innumerable attributes,
    each of which is a "lamp of fire"
    enlightening the soul and communicating the warmth of love.

1.   To expound the mystical life is itself a mystical grace. It is
       one thing to experience it, another to "explain the unexplainable.
       Mystical wisdom, which comes through love, need not be
       understood distinctly" (S.C. *Prologue* 1). St. Teresa speaks of
       this in *The Life*, chapter XII; we tread on holy ground. In this
       stanza the Saint reflects on the work of the Holy Spirit in us
       to bring us to a mystical understanding of the attributes of
       God. These in turn are communicated by God's loving action
       to the soul, which participates in God. "It will be necessary
       here that the Holy Spirit guide the pen of the writer" (S.C. 26.1).

       "O lamps of fire !"::

2.   The "attributes" of God are all those qualities of goodness,
       mercy, justice, power, which our human minds "attribute" to
       Him. God *is* love, God *is* wisdom, God *is* mercy; we do not
       simply say, "God is loving, wise, merciful." The participation
       of the soul in God extends even to a sharing in and acquiring
       the very attributes of God, "each of which is the very being
       of God." As it receives, so it gives; it is enlightened, and it
       enlightens others. Love is communicated from God, who is
       love, and this love is in turn shared, communicated, to others
       (similarly for wisdom, goodness, justice, mercy, and all God's
       attributes).

3.   The soul has a clear knowledge of each of God's attributes,
        and enjoys a sharing, or participation in them,
        both singly and collectively.
        Each one, and altogether, are received
        in one act of loving union.
        God Himself is for the soul many lamps together,
        each of which illumines and imparts warmth;
        it is inflamed by love through its clear knowledge of each one.
        The many lamps shine and burn as one.
        The soul, in loving each one, loves also through all together.
        Light and warmth of love are communicated
        according to each separate attribute,
        whether it be omnipotence, wisdom, goodness, justice, mercy . . .
        Thus God communicates Himself to the soul as one,
        but in and through each single attribute.

4.   When God passed by on Mount Sinai
        Moses beheld these lamps, or attributes of God—
        omnipotence, power, His Godhead, mercy,
        justice, truth, righteousness.
        He experienced sublime enjoyment
        begotten of infused, loving knowledge.

5.   The delight experienced in this rapture of love
        comes from all the attributes together, and from each singly.
        Each single attribute, aflame with love,
        lights up and inflames the other;
        and all together make one light and one fire.
        Aglow, inflamed with this all-consuming love,
        the soul sees clearly that eternal life is in loving.

3.   St. John touches on this in *The Spiritual Canticle* (S.C. 37.7);
        here he elaborates. Astonishing as it may seem, so intimate
        is the union with God, so complete the transformation of the
        soul in God, "each seeming to be the other", that the soul
        has a distinct knowledge of its own participation in God's
        attributes. And this not only in a general way, but with distinct
        awareness of each single attribute, as being its own.

4.   Moses experienced a sublime insight into God's power and
        dominion, but most of all into His mercy: "Emperor, Lord, God,
        merciful, clement, patient, of much compassion, true, giving
        mercy unto thousands, who takes away iniquities and sins; no
        one is innocent in your sight" (Ex. 34:6-7). It is God Himself,
        not Moses, who proclaimed His name (Lord : Yahweh)—then
        proclaimed His attributes. This differs somewhat from St. John's
        reading of the text. He says, "Moses began to call out and
        enumerate some of God's attributes."

5.   In receiving and participating in each attribute of God, and
        in all together as one, the soul, aware as never before of God's
        love, in this undreamt-of sharing of His very life, is overwhelmed
        by love, and experiences an insight into what eternal life is:
        love alone, love experienced, realized, yielding up all its secrets
        eternally; a never-ending and always-renewed sounding of the
        height and depth of God's love for us. ("Its delight is the delight
        of God" (L.F. II.34). Now the soul understands: "Eternal life
        is knowing you, the only true God, and Jesus Christ, whom
        you have sent" (Jn. 17:3); "God is love" (1 Jn. 4:8).

6.   When we love and do good to others,
         we do so according to our nature and attributes.
         So, God, dwelling in us, loves us,
         and grants us His favors according to His nature.
         As the omnipotent, He loves us and does good to us
         omnipotently;
         as the All Wise, He loves us and does good to us with wisdom—
         so for His goodness, holiness, justice, mercy, truth, and so on.
         He rejoices in this loving union, making the soul His equal.

7.   The experience of being so loved and esteemed by God
         is inexpressible; it beggars description.
         Both soul and body have become a paradise,
         watered divinely, joyously, by an impetuous river of living water.

8.   The light and fire of God is so gentle
         that it could be compared also with living waters
         which satisfy the thirst of the spirit.
         The spirit of God, hidden in the depths of the soul,
         is gently satisfying, like soft, refreshing water
         in its strong impetus of love towards God.
         It resembles a living flame, or "lamp" of fire.
         Since the transformation of the soul in God is indescribable,
         everything we have said falls short of the reality.
         The soul becomes God from God
         by participation in Him and in His attributes,
         which it terms "lamps of fire."

9.   *in whose splendors*:

         These "splendors" are the loving knowledge
         which the lamps of God's attributes give forth to the soul.
         Material lamps give their light outwardly,
         playing only on the surface of an object.
         These lamps transform and enlighten inwardly,
         as air within the flame is enkindled and transformed
         into the flame itself.

6.   God can love in only one way—infinitely, without measure.
       It is His nature to give of Himself. Being All Goodness, He
       "diffuses" goodness, and the soul, disposed by love, receives
       according to each attribute. Besides those mentioned, St. John
       speaks of God's mildness, clemency, strength, sublimity,
       delicacy, purity, liberality, humility ("supreme" humility). St.
       John speaks of "the lamp of rigorous justice" of God which
       passed by Abraham (Gen. 15:12, 17); but now, he says, "all
       the lamps of the knowledge of God illumine you with a pleasant
       and loving light." God speaks to us, with rejoicing: "I am yours
       and for you and I am delighted to be what I am so that I can
       be yours and give myself to you" (*text*).

7.   St. John cites Scripture: Ex.7:2, Ps. 44:9, Song of Songs 4:15,
       Ps. 45:5. The Bride is overwhelmed by the gift of the knowledge
       of the Bridegroom's graces and virtues, which become her own.
       She is as though inundated by life-giving, vehement waters of
       love.

8.   St. John says that the lamps of fire are living waters of the
       spirit, like those that descended on the Apostles (cf. Acts 2:3).
       "I will pour out upon you clean waters and . . . will put my
       spirit in the midst of you" (Ez. 36:25–27). He then partially
       clarifies the confusion of the two mixed metaphors of fire and
       water by citing 2 Macc. 1:20–22; Nehemiah (not Jeremiah—
       see text) ordered water to be sprinkled on the fire which had
       been secretly hidden: "A great fire blazed up, so that everyone
       marvelled." This concludes the section (commencing para. 2)
       on God's attributes, and the soul's sharing, or participation in
       them. St. John uses the word *indecible*—not to be said even,
       much less described.

9.   "A flame," says St. John, "is nothing but enkindled air." The
       figure of speech is exact, and says all. Both air and flame become
       one; God and the soul become one in shared, loving knowledge
       of each other, a sharing of God's attributes.

10.   The movements of the divine flame
       are the work of both the Holy Spirit and the soul.
       Just as the flame flickers together with the air it has enkindled,
       thus bringing the air nearer to itself,
       so the Holy Spirit absorbs the soul into itself,
       until it enters into the perfect life in Christ.

11.   These "movements" are of the soul, not of God,
       for God does not "move" in Himself.
       The soul "moves" only because of its imperfection.
       The glimpses of glory it receives, however,
       are stable, perfect, and continuous,
       as they will be in the soul hereafter.

12.   These splendors may also be called "overshadowings."
       Casting a shadow over another signifies protection,
       befriending, or granting favors,
       just as the Blessed Virgin was "overshadowed"
       by the Holy Spirit (Luke 1:35).

13.   Everything casts a shadow in proportion to its nature and size.
       A dark object casts a dark shadow;
       a light, fine object casts a light, fine shadow;
       long or short, according to its length.

14.   So when the lamp of God's beauty casts a shadow,
       the shadow will partake of God's beauty,
       or of His wisdom, or strength, as the case may be.
       In shadow: the partaking in this life is imperfect,
       since the soul's comprehension is limited.
       Yet it is a real and effective realization
       of the excellence and attributes of God—
       that is, of God Himself.
       In this sense "splendors" could be called "shadows."

10.   Both flame and air need each other, but "the soul is so moved
       by the Spirit of God that all its operations are divine" (Asc.
       III: 2.16). Absorption, not annihilation: the Spirit, which as St.
       Irenaeus says, "would ready us for God" (*Paraclitus qui nos
       aptaret Deo*) prepares the way for perfect union in Christ.

11.   The wavering of the flame is compared to the soul's
       imperfection. "Afterwards"—that is, in heaven—all will be
       stillness, without movement, and the glimpses of God
       "constantly serene." The flame may flicker and waver, but the
       fire itself, in its deepest center, does not move.

12.   The metaphor changes—from "lamps" (God's attributes) to
       "casting a shadow." The text from St. Luke is: "The Holy Spirit
       will come upon you and the power of the Most High will
       overshadow you." The Apostles were "overshadowed" by the
       bright cloud at the Transfiguration.

13.   St. John, referring back to "in whose splendors", calls them
       "overshadowings of great splendor." This may seem
       contradictory, but we might recall the "luminous cloud" of the
       Transfiguration which "overshadowed" the Apostles; "luminous
       cloud" is a seeming contradiction also.

14.   Despite the soul's limitations, the soul really "enjoys God
       according to His likeness and measure in each of the shadows."
       The Saint sums it up: "To express it better: it will be the very
       wisdom, and the very beauty, and the very fortitude of God
       in shadow, because the soul cannot comprehend God
       perfectly . . . the soul clearly knows God's excellence."

15.   So when God casts the shadows
      of His own virtues and attributes,
      the soul understands and experiences Him in each of them:
      divine power in the shadow of omnipotence,
      divine wisdom in the shadow of wisdom,
      infinite goodness in the shadow of goodness,
      and so on for all the attributes;
      in short, the glory of God in the shadow of glory.
      Each bright, enkindled lamp
      casts its own bright and enkindled shadow,
      each being part of one single lamp
      in the one single, simple Being of God.

16.   Just as Ezechiel saw the beast with four faces,
      and the wheel with four wheels,
      under the appearance of kindled coals and lamps,
      signifying the wisdom of God
      and the many grandeurs of God,
      so the soul has distinct knowledge
      of God passing through it in one single sound
      and sees itself to be exalted
      in beauty far beyond all telling.

17.   So the soul has come to understand
      that through the purity of divine wisdom,
      many things are seen when one is seen.
      This divine wisdom which is Christ
      is the storehouse of the treasures of the Father,
      the splendor of eternal light,
      a stainless mirror and image of His goodness.

15.   The seeming and perhaps labored repetition emphasizes, on the one hand, God's infinite condescension in sharing Himself in and through the very sharing of His attributes and, on the other, the finiteness, the limitation of the soul. Despite the infinite distance, God's love is great enough to bridge the gap. By the action of the Holy Spirit the soul really participates in the simple Being of God, in and through its sharing in each of His attributes, which the soul, in a sense, appropriates.

16.   This paragraph is difficult; the whole passage from Ezechiel (1:5–28) should be read. It is the inaugural vision of Ezechiel of the chariot of the glory of God, the chariot symbolising the divine attributes. The chariot is many-winged, many-wheeled, many-eyed, capable of moving in any direction instantly, flashing the fire of God's holiness, a fire which consumes all that is unholy. The four living figures, or cherubim, which bore the throne, or chariot, of God passed by to the "sound of wings, loud as waters in flood or thunder from on high." Ezechiel's theme: the transcendence, the "wholly other" nature of God.

17.   St. John does not mention the name of Christ, but it is clear that he is addressing Christ: "By your purity, O divine Wisdom, many things are seen in you when one is seen. For you are the deposit of the Father's treasures." The divine attributes are "seen and enjoyed distinctly, each one is enkindled as the other, and each is substantially the other" in Christ, the Wisdom of God.

18.   *"the deep caverns of feeling":*

These "caverns" are the faculties of the soul—
memory, understanding, and will—
"deep" because of their infinite depth and capacity;
capable of being filled with the infinite.
They must be completely empty
of what is not God
before they can be filled with the fullness of God.
When they are empty and cleansed completely
they experience an intolerable yearning for God.
This commonly occurs toward the close
of the soul's purification and illumination.
Just before it attains to fullness of union,
having glimpsed the divine, yet being deprived of it,
it suffers with impatient love,
which is worse than death.

19.   The understanding's emptiness is the thirst for God,
compared with the vehement thirst of the hart
for living waters (Ps.42.1).
It thirsts for the wisdom of God,
which is the object of the understanding.

20.   The second cavern is the will
which hungers for the perfection of love.
"My soul longs and faints for the courts of the Lord" (Ps.83).

21.   The third cavern is the memory,
which is emptied, or dispossessed,
in order to make way for the possession of God.

18.   "The deep caverns of [sense]", proposed in some translations, can hardly be accurate. The Saint is simply restating the need to "empty" the faculties, or powers of the soul, in the dark night of the spirit—"this blessed night which brings darkness to the spirit in order to flood it with light." It is not always conscious of "a burning and anxious love" and "this loving light of the dark night of contemplation sometimes acts more upon the will and sometimes more in the intellect" (D.N. II:12 . 5, 7).

19.   This is John's interpretation; Psalm 42 makes no reference to wisdom (living waters). "God's wisdom is so limitless, immense, as to be incomprehensible; the soul can always penetrate further into the mystery of the knowledge of God" (S.C. 36.10).

20.   Hunger, intense longing for God, desire to love Him more and more, without limit—unmistakable signs of being "drawn" by God. The "drawing" is not necessarily *felt*; the interplay of intellect and will is clearly illustrated in *The Dark Night* (II. 12.5–7): "the will . . . is marvellously set aglow as though a living flame set it alight with a living fire of living understanding."

21.   St. John's teaching on hope in the memory is recalled, as in *The Ascent*, III:1.15, and *The Dark Night*, II:9.5, and II:21.6–9: "Empty of all possession and support, it neither sees nor cares for anything but God alone." Cf. Lamentations 3:20: "My soul shall melt within me . . . I shall live in hope of God."

22.   These caverns are "deep", containing the infinite;
       for the faculties have the capacity for containing God.
       So their hunger, thirst, languishing, and pain are infinite—
       a kind of endless death.
       This suffering is a kind of image
       of the suffering of the next life,
       since the soul is now disposed to receive the fullness of God,
       but it cannot do so.
       In the next life, the suffering is in the will,
       in privation of love, which cannot lessen the pain.
       For the greater the love, the greater the impatience
       for the possession of God, who is desired so intensely.

23.   When the soul desires God with such intensity
       it already possesses Him whom it loves;
       how then can it be yearning for Him?
       As for the angels, their desire to possess God
       brings them only delight, and never satiety.
       So the greater the soul's delight in God,
       the greater its desire for Him—
       greater than the suffering and pain
       of not fully possessing Him.

24.   We should note clearly the difference
       between the possession of God through grace alone
       and the possession of Him through union.
       In the first, through grace alone, there is deep, mutual love.
       In the second, through union, there is also communication.
       The first is to the second as betrothal is to marriage.
       Betrothal is consent by agreement, unity of will; not union.
       Marriage means communication, and union of the persons.
       So we are speaking (para. 23) of betrothal—
       possession of God not through union but through grace.
       The will is cleansed of tastes and desires;
       the will of the soul and the will of God are one,
       and the Bridegroom makes loving visits,
       causing intense delight.

22.   The faculties have the potential for "containing God", since God has infused Faith, Hope, and Love, the only means of possessing Him in this life—but never as perfectly as in the Beatific Vision. "Although in Spiritual Marriage there is not the perfection of heavenly love, there is nonetheless a living and totally ineffable semblance of that perfection" (S.C. 38.4). Not yet able to possess God perfectly, the soul suffers. St. John likens this suffering to that of purgatory. There the suffering consists in the deprivation of God, now known and loved but not possessed, though vehemently desired above all else. The Saint reminds us that he is speaking of the time "toward the close of the soul's purification and illumination, just before it attains to fullness of union."

23.   The Saint poses the question, and the answer is contained in the following paragraph. The soul possesses God, but not fully. There is a certain pain in this possession, borne of awareness that it is not the full possession of God. But the desire and the delight which result from it outweigh the pain of not fully possessing God.

24.   The Saint's thought is now clarified. The yearning is that of betrothal, hoping for fulfillment in marriage. Love alone, or consent only, or agreement of wills cannot satisfy; only full union in marriage. "Possession" is delightful in betrothal, but it is not yet full possession, as in marriage, of the beloved. These intense desires are experienced in the Sixth Mansions of St. Teresa: "The more the soul learns about . . . God, the more her desire increases. . . . Her desires become so great as to cause her great distress" (I.C. Mans. VI.11). For presence of God in (1) essence, (2) grace, (3) love, see *The Spiritual Canticle*, 11.3.

25.   These delights are not marriage, but preparation for it.
Although the soul is greatly purified in this state of betrothal,
still more positive preparations are needed for marriage.
God has to purify it further by loving visits and gifts,
as the young maidens chosen by King Ahasuerus
were first prepared by precious ointments of myrrh and spices.

26.   During this time of expectation of marriage,
the anointings of the Holy Spirit are more sublime.
The longing anxieties of the soul are extreme and delicate
and the desire for union is more profound and delicate.

27.   Those on whom God bestows these delicate anointings
would be well advised to take care as to how they act,
and to remember into whose hands they commit themselves.
The great harm caused by losing the effects of these anointings
must at all costs be avoided.
Though warning them and advising them in this regard
means digressing from our main theme,
we shall soon return to it.

28.   If a soul is seeking God,
the Beloved is seeking it much more;
if the soul directs its loving desires to God,
He sends "the fragrance of ointments"—
His divine touches and inspirations—
by which He "draws it, and makes it run after Him."
It is God who gives this desire for Himself,
preparing the soul so delicately
that it merits union with Him
and substantial transformation in all its faculties.

29.   We should always remember that God is the principal agent.
He is like the guide to a blind man
leading him to a place he could not otherwise reach—
to supernatural things beyond its natural capacity.
The blind man must place no obstacle in the guide's way,
such as allowing himself to be guided by another blind man.
For the soul seeking union with God
this might be a spiritual director or the devil or itself.

25. Here there is some discrepancy in the numbering of paragraphs in the various translations, but all the texts are substantially the same. Note: "God has to purify it further." The preparation for marriage and the purification still necessary are God's work. The young maidens (Est. 2:12) were first chosen, then prepared. See paragraph 26 below: the "anointings" are the work of the Holy Spirit.

26. St. John says, "The desire for God is the preparation for union with Him." In *The Spiritual Canticle* we read: "God does not give grace and love except according to the soul's desire and love. The more the soul desires and loves, the more God gives" (S.C. 13.12); "Hence, the importance of greatly desiring the divine breeze of the Holy Spirit, and of asking for it" (17.9).

27. The Saint is firm in his intention to digress from the subject of "the deep caverns of feeling" and to give practical advice as to how to proceed when God gives these "delicate anointings" lest the good effect be lost. The "digression" runs to forty paragraphs; the theme of "caverns" is taken up again in paragraph 68. The next forty paragraphs are a splendid résumé of St. John's teaching on prayer.

28. The "column of smoke, the breathing of myrrh and frankincense", the "fragrance of His ointments by which He draws it and makes it run after Him" (*text*), are clear references to the Song of Songs, 3:6, and 1:3. The soul "merits" union, because by God's gift alone it has become pleasing to Him: "The bride is anxious that nothing be attributed to her; it was His favor in gazing on her that transformed her; her merit comes from this alone" (S.C. 32:2).

29. A blind man must trust his guide, absolutely, and not do anything to impede the guide. St. John never ceases reminding us that only God begins, continues, and completes our sanctification. The soul can freely and deliberately put obstacles in God's way: listening to unwise spiritual direction, yielding to the devil's temptations, or reverting to self-centeredness.

30. It is very important in seeking spiritual direction,
   to choose carefully the person
   to whom we are entrusting the guidance of our soul.
   It will be difficult to find a spiritual guide
   who is at once learned, discreet, and experienced.
   Not many understand the intermediary stages,
   much less the higher ways of the spiritual life.
   While knowledge and discretion are the foundation,
   the director himself must needs have experienced
   the things of the Spirit
   if he is to succeed in leading the soul onwards.

31. Many spiritual directors do a great deal of harm.
   Since they do not understand the ways of the Spirit,
   they cause souls to lose the unction of the Holy Spirit.
   They direct them in the only way they know,
   that which pertains to beginners (if they know even this),
   not permitting them to go beyond discursive, imaginative prayer,
   whereas God wants them to pass beyond it.

32. Beginners should be encouraged to meditate,
   make discursive reflection, and use the imagination.
   By making interior acts of love they profit spiritually
   and gradually acquire a taste for spiritual things
   as a result of the delight and satisfaction felt in the senses.
   When this happens
   and the soul has acquired fortitude and constancy,
   God begins to wean it, so to speak,
   and to place it in the state of contemplation.
   This can happen quickly if the soul is well disposed.
   It no longer enjoys sensible satisfaction in reflections,
   and finds itself unable to practice meditation as before.
   There is no joy in it, only dryness in the senses.
   The soul's main activity has passed from sense to spirit.
   In this new experience, God gives, the soul receives;
   it is the gift of contemplation, or loving knowledge
   without particular acts on the part of the soul.

30.   St. John does not say simply "'It is important to have a spiritual
       director"; he chooses his words more carefully. Having a
       spiritual director is important—but the Saint's implication is
       that it is better not to have *any* spiritual director if the director
       with the necessary qualities cannot be found. He sees it as
       necessary, not just desirable, that the director have personal
       experience of the higher ways of the mystical life. Many, however,
       who undertook the direction of St. Teresa lacked this experience.
       Perhaps she is less demanding; for her thoughts on spiritual
       direction see *The Life* 5.3, 13.14, and I.C. Mans. V.1, VI.8, VII.11.

31.   Incompetent directors place an obstacle to the action of the
       Holy Spirit: "They cause souls to lose the unction of the delicate
       ointments with which the Holy Spirit gradually anoints and
       prepares them for Himself" (*text*). Great sensitivity to the Spirit's
       action, enlightened discernment, are needed. The director must
       always keep in mind that the "principal director is the Holy
       Spirit" (L.F. 3.46).

32.   No other spiritual writer has such a clear analysis of the
       "passage" from meditation to contemplation. The transition
       from one to the other is a phase of the great ascending movement
       from sense to spirit. There is no minimizing of the importance
       of meditation, of using the mind and the imagination, in the
       first stages: "They [the reflections] serve as a means to beginners
       to dispose and habituate the spirit to spirituality by means of
       sense." They are "like stairs, merely a means of reaching the
       top"; it is necessary to pass through them and have done with
       them since they have no proportion to the goal to which they
       lead" (Asc. II.5).

33.   Directors, discerning this change from sense to spirit,
        should encourage such souls not to stay in meditation,
        and not to seek or desire devotional feelings of fervor.
        Trying to meditate causes only distraction
        and loss of recollection.
        God is secretly infusing loving wisdom and knowledge,
        usually without specific acts.
        The soul has only to remain passive,
        in simple loving awareness,
        not depending on its own efforts,
        as a person simply opens his eyes with loving attention.

34.   Since God communes with us by means of simple, loving
        knowledge,
        we who receive commune with Him in the same way.
        Knowledge is joined to knowledge, love with love.
        If we receive in a purely natural manner,
        we are incapable of receiving the supernatural.
        If, instead of remaining receptive and tranquil,
        we insist on making natural acts,
        we hinder God's action
        in communicating with us supernaturally in loving knowledge,
        purifying us, at first interiorly,
        afterwards in the delight of love.
        To receive this loving knowledge is to receive passively
        according to the way God gives it—supernaturally.
        We should remain quiet, peaceful, serene, receptive,
        adapting quietly to God's way, not our own.
        The purer the air, the brighter the sunshine.
        We should not cling to anything
        either to our own way of meditation,
        or to any satisfaction or consolation in prayer.
        Thus we free ourselves of anything which may cause disquiet,
        or disturb the deep silence of senses and spirit
        in which we listen with deep, sensitive awareness.

35.   We will recognize this state of loving knowledge
        by the accompanying peace, tranquility, and inward absorption.
        We should then make no effort to practice loving awareness;
        rather we should remain free for whatever the Lord desires,
        conscious only of being placed in this solitude
        and in a state of simply listening.

33.   One should consult *The Ascent*, Book II, chapters 8–14, where St. John speaks of the nature of "loving wisdom and knowledge" infused by God. It is so "delicate, spiritual and interior that the soul does not perceive or feel it, even though employed in it . . . the purer, simpler and more perfect it is, the darker it seems to be and the less the intellect perceives." Some translations render *sin hacer de suyo diligencias* as "without efforts of its own", which could be misleading. The Saint has already said "without specific acts." Whereas before, in making meditation, we built up ideas, concepts, to feed the imagination and the mind, now we make the effort of quietly putting them aside in order to let God act freely. There always remains "effort" on our part, no matter how exalted our prayer. "Opening the eyes" requires "effort", minimal though it may be.

34.   St. John quotes: "Whatever is received is received in the recipient according to the manner of acting of the one who receives." The emphasis here is on our receptivity to God's action. Our "simple loving knowledge" must be completely divested of thoughts, ideas, or imagining. These are the tools of natural knowledge, and have no place here: "enfolded in divine love, a divine calm and peace pervade the soul, and we enter into wonderful, sublime knowledge of God" (Asc. II:15.5). But, St. John notes, "this general knowledge [contemplation] of which we speak is at times so subtle and delicate that we can neither realize it, nor perceive it; it shines like a light, so purely and simply in the intellect that the soul does not perceive its presence. We have received the supernatural knowledge which is contemplation" (Asc. II: 14 . 8, 10, 11).

35.   Like Mary of Bethany at the feet of Jesus (Luke 10:38–42) we are in a state of listening, totally receptive, not even making the effort at "loving awareness." We "learn to be still in God. Little by little, but very quickly, we become enfolded in divine love; we enter into wonderful, sublime knowledge of God . . . we discover that God is God" (Asc. II:15.5).

36.   Once having entered this simple, restful state of contemplation,
        we should not engage in meditations or seek spiritual
        consolation.
        We should, rather, stand firmly on our feet,
        in detachment from everything.
        Pure contemplation is in receiving.

37.   This highest wisdom and language of God—contemplation—
        can be received only in silence,
        with detachment from use of the mind
        and from the desire for personal gratification.

38.   It is the task of the spiritual director to bring the soul
        into complete withdrawal and solitude.
        The more it is detached from its own satisfaction,
        and from pleasure in reflecting on spiritual things,
        from all care and anxiety about things of heaven or of earth,
        the more copiously will the spirit of Divine Wisdom
        be infused into the soul.
        This wisdom is loving, tranquil, peaceful, inebriating;
        the soul is tenderly and gently wounded without knowing how.

39.   Even a little of this holy restfulness and solitude
        is an inestimable blessing,
        and though we are not always conscious of its benefits,
        we will come to understand in due time.
        There will be a marked preference for solitude;
        what is merely worldly will be distasteful and wearisome
        now that we have tasted this gentleness
        of life and love in the spirit.

40.   The Holy Spirit gives these delicate, hidden unctions
        and, without our realizing it,
        we are being filled with spiritual riches, gifts, and graces.
        These are gifts of God, who gives only as God.

36.   St. John quotes Habakuk 2:1 — "I will stand on my watchtower, and take up my post on my battlements, watching to see what he will say to me"—to emphasize the firmness and determination with which we should raise the mind above activity and natural knowledge in order to receive pure contemplation. Here and elsewhere in this section, St. John uses the term *ocioso*, which literally means "idle". Perhaps "restful" is a better rendering; "idle" has unfortunate overtones in English.

37.   Quoting Isaiah 28:9, St. John draws the following inference: only those who are "weaned from the milk" (of satisfaction) and "drawn from the breasts" (of particular knowledge) will receive the pure knowledge of God. St. Teresa: "Let us not perplex our understanding in trying to understand something that is from God" (I.C. Mans. V.1).

38.   The operation of the senses and of the mind is a kind of slavery. As the Chosen People were liberated and entered the Promised Land, so we experience a new freedom, the infusion of divine wisdom, free of "all care and anxiety about heavenly things!" (*text*).

39.   The desire for solitude is the most important of the three signs given by St. John to indicate that God is calling us to remain in general, loving awareness of Him, without particular acts. The new knowledge of God is secret: "God secretly teaches and instructs it in the perfection of love without its understanding of what manner is this infused contemplation." We do not understand what is happening, but we do arrive at awareness that God is acting in us in a new and special way. (For the "three signs", cf. Asc II.12, D.N. I.9.)

40.   It is the work of the Holy Spirit: "You cannot tell where it comes from or where it is going" (Jn. 3:8). God can give in only one way, infinitely, as God: "If only you knew the gift of God!" (Jn. 4:10).

41.   These delicate and sublime anointings of the Holy Spirit
        are so refined and pure
        that neither the soul nor the director understands them.
        The least acts of the memory, intellect, or will,
        or any use of the senses, or desires for one's satisfaction
        would be a disturbance and a hindrance.

42.   The harm done by interference with these holy unctions
        can be compared to the incalculable damage done
        if a portrait of extremely delicate workmanship
        were to be daubed with dull, unpleasing colours
        by an unskilled hand.
        The delicacy of the Holy Spirit's artistry
        would be irreparably marred by such interference.

43.   There is hardly any spiritual director
        who does not fail in this.
        How often God anoints a true contemplative
        with the delicate unction of loving, serene, peaceful knowledge,
        so that meditation or reflection becomes impossible,
        and along comes a so-called spiritual director
        who, like a blacksmith, knows only how to meditate
        and to hammer and pound with the faculties.
        And he advises them: "Enough of this foolishness;
        do your part, make interior acts, exercise the mind.
        Enough of this quietude and rest;
        it's just idleness, waste of time, full of illusions."

44.   These directors, lacking understanding, are not aware
        that in contemplation God speaks secretly to the soul
        and that the use of the senses and discursive reflection
        are no longer necessary or desirable—
        are harmful, in fact, and cause only distraction.

45.   These directors understand neither recollection nor solitude,
        both of which are lost when they insist on natural activity
        when they should be letting God work supernaturally.
        They are hammering the horseshoe instead of the nail.

41.   We are reminded of St. John's frequent references to contemplation: "God secretly teaches and instructs it without it understanding how. It is secret wisdom communicated and infused. Secret wisdom—secret and hidden from the very one who receives it." And directors take note: "Nor does the director understand them!"

42.   St. John suggests also that the interference (on the part of a director) would do immeasurably greater harm than that done in the direction of many "ordinary souls", so great is the value to the church of one person who is drawn to divine intimacy by the Holy Spirit. The director must realize that the real director is the Holy Spirit (see S.C. 29.3).

43.   Directors, take note. One senses a certain exasperation in St. John, as though he had in mind true contemplatives, who had suffered at the hands of inexperienced, unlearned directors. The pity of it is that such directors cause the soul to go backwards rather than to progress in divine union, thus hindering the action of the Holy Spirit.

44.   The soul "has already reached the negation and silence of the senses and of meditation and has come to the way of the spirit, which is contemplation." Repeating the exercise is useless: the goal has been attained. The purpose of the meditation was to dispose the soul for contemplation.

45.   The Saint speaks of the "sublime unctions" which God produces in the soul in recollection and solitude. This is a "lofty work" of God, fashioning His own image in the soul. All is to no avail if we revert to using our own natural ways—discursive activity, meditation, use of the mind. And worse still, "the director may prescribe elementary spiritual exercises."

46.   Directors are merely instruments of the Holy Spirit,
         the principal guide and director of souls.
         They should not impose their own ideas,
         but try to discern what God is doing,
         leaving the soul completely, if they cannot do this.
         What the soul needs is greater solitude,
         tranquillity, and freedom of spirit
         in which there is no anxiety about seeming to do nothing,
         in recognition of the fact that God is doing everything.
         A good director aims to free the soul
         and to lead it to desire true spiritual poverty,
         and to let go particular knowledge and ideas
         and desire for satisfaction and pleasure,
         in complete dispossession of the desire for spiritual things.
         The soul must do this with the director's guidance
         God will then unfailingly do His part,
         communicating Himself in silence, secretly,
         as surely as the sunlight enters into a room
         which is opened up to the light.

47.   God stands ready to communicate Himself.
         Directors simply dispose souls for this,
         their only task being to prepare them
         for the nakedness and dispossession of both sense and spirit
         according to the demands of the Gospel.
         They should not think the soul is not advancing
         because it seems to be doing nothing.
         By such "doing nothing" it is accomplishing a great deal,
         freeing itself of particular knowledge
         and acts of the understanding.

48.   The soul reaches God more by not-knowing than by knowing.
         Particular knowledge and ideas give way to faith,
         through emptying of everything that can be grasped by the mind,
         for God cannot be confined within human knowledge
         nor within a heart given to wrongful affections.
         The soul is right to desire to remain in idleness,
         and if it lets go of ideas, it advances in faith,
         which cannot of itself understand the nature of God.
         In submission, it surrenders its desire to know.

46. St. John does not use the term "spiritual director." Rather, he says "spiritual master" (*maestro*), "spiritual father" or, simply, "guide" (*guía*) or "director" (*agente*). This is one who (1) trains in detachment by directing all the faculties to God in faith, hope and love, (2) discerns and evaluates the soul's religious experience and growth in prayer, and (3) supports with understanding and compassion during "dark" periods of trial, aridity, dryness of spirit. Above all, "he must lead souls in God's way, not his own." The real director is the Holy Spirit. The director's very positive role is to lead the soul to the desire to be purified by God of wrongful desires, and St. John includes, in this complete dispossession, desires for spiritual favors or graces as well as the more obvious desires for worldly possessions. If the soul is so disposed, St. John says, "it is impossible that God will fail to do His part."

47. Paragraphs 47 and 48 should be read with Book II of *The Ascent* in mind, especially chapters 4–10, in which the Saint treats of the active night of the spirit. "Keep in mind," he says, "that I am addressing those who have begun to enter the state of contemplation." It is precisely this that the director must recognize. The director should be conversant with St. John's teaching on the "passage", or transition, to a simplified way of contemplative prayer (see L.F. 3.33 and, in particular, Asc. II. 12, 13, 14, 15; D.N. I.9; and *Maxims and Counsels* 40).

48. From *The Ascent*: "Faith . . . imparts new knowledge of something never before experienced. Our understanding of natural things is blinded in the glare of faith's illumination. In acquiring this supernatural knowledge we do not use our intellect at all—it has no power to grasp the supernatural. In the delights of pure contemplation . . . faith alone is our guide. In faith, we enter within ourselves, to find God, and in this way, of faith alone, we are marvellously enlightened" (Asc. II.3, 4).

49.   It is true that in the natural operations of the soul
the will does not love except what the intellect understands.
But in contemplation (which we are discussing),
by which God infuses Himself into the soul,
particular acts of knowledge are unnecessary
because God communicates light and love together
in a loving knowledge which is supernatural.
This knowledge enkindles love as light also transmits heat.
This contemplative knowledge is as darkness to the intellect—
darkness which is also light, a ray of darkness.
Both the love and the knowledge of God are dark,
since according to the understanding they lack clarity.
God may touch and inflame in a special way
now the intellect, with knowledge, now the will, with love,
inflaming it with the warmth of His love
without its understanding how.

50.   God can and does make acts of love in the soul
which are much more delightful than its own acts.
These acts inebriate it with infused love of contemplation.
God enkindles it, moving and taking hold of it in love.
There is no need to feel that the will is in idleness.

51.   God infuses this love in the will,
provided that it is free of other pleasurable affections,
and the soul can be sure it is advancing
even though it feels no particular experience of God.
There is enjoyment of God, but it may be secret and obscure.
Now nothing satisfies it as much as solitary quietude,
which is a sign that it loves God above all things.
In nakedness and emptiness of all other tastes and desires,
it goes forward to God, who is otherwise inaccessible.
It is not surprising that it does not feel Him.

52.   Since God cannot be grasped
by forms and figures in the imagination,
the memory walks safely in not relying on them.

53.   Some directors know nothing of this quiet contemplation,
having never experienced it themselves.
They cause great grief, affliction, and dryness of spirit
by insisting on meditation, reflection, and interior acts
when they should be advising just the opposite.

49.   "Mystical wisdom, which comes through love, need not be understood distinctly ... We love God, in faith, without understanding Him" (S.C. Prologue 2). The sun, in giving light, also generates heat, so this new supernatural knowledge enkindles love, in one act of loving knowledge, which, being beyond the power of the natural intellect, is darkness to it; light and darkness in one act. St. John borrows the phrase "ray of darkness" from the *Mystica Theologia* of Dionysius Areopagita (used also in D.N. 5, S.C. 14, 15.16). Yet "this knowledge ... is very delightful to the intellect, since it is a knowledge belonging to the intellect, and it is delightful to the will since it is communicated in love, which pertains to the will" (cf. S.C. 27,5).

50.   "These acts of love are most precious; one of them is more meritorious and valuable than all the deeds a person may have performed in His whole life without this transformation—such is the activity of the Holy Spirit in the soul transformed in love" (*text* 1.3).

51.   This paragraph is helpful and enlightening to those who may still be equating this infusion of love with some pleasurable or consoling experience. The Saint suggests that ordinarily it will not be so, since in the nature of things, God is inaccessible. The desire and preference for silence, quiet, and solitude is a sign that all is well, that the soul is advancing, even to loving Him above all things.

52.   At this stage we place no importance on what we can imagine about God. The memory must be purified of these imaginings.

53.   In this case, there is no substitute for experience. Directors should know that discursive meditation has no purpose other than to dispose us for the grace of contemplation; it is not an end in itself. These directors, the Saint says, "even persuade souls to strive for satisfaction and feelings of fervor"—the exact opposite of what they should be doing.

81

54.   This is to intrude roughly on the work of God,
        who places high value on the work He has done
        in bringing the soul to this solitude of the heart
        in which He speaks to it in peace and rest.

55.   In the Song of Songs 3:5, God indicates
        how much He loves this solitary restfulness,
        citing the roes and harts, which love solitude.
        By contrast, the little foxes (Song of Songs 2:15)
        destroy the flourishing vineyard of the soul.

56.   Even though they know no better
        it is grievously wrong for directors
        to meddle roughly in what they do not understand.
        It is their duty to know, and to show sensitivity
        where matters of infinite loss or gain are in question.

57.   There is no excuse for vanity in this matter.
        No director should think he knows everything,
        nor should he refuse
        to let the soul choose another spiritual road.
        In making a statue, not everyone is capable
        of hewing the wood, carving the statue,
        polishing and painting, and putting the finishing touches.
        Each workman has his own special task,
        and his own limitations.

58.   So no director should think he is so perfect
        as to have all the skills required for direction,
        and there may come a time when the soul needs someone else.
        The statue will never be completed
        if all we can do is hammer and hew the wood.
        We should allow God to complete the work.

59.   It is impossible that one director
        should have all the qualities required to guide every soul.
        All souls are different; God leads each one by different paths.
        To presume otherwise is tyranny in a director,
        not to speak of a pride and presumption that leads to jealousy.

60.   God is very angry with directors such as this,
        as we read in the prophet Ezechiel 34:3–10.

54.   These directors seem incapable of recognizing that God has
       taken over the work of direction; the soul is to be encouraged
       to be receptive, to listen to God speaking in the heart.

55.   Song of Songs 3:5: "I adjure you, daughters of Jerusalem, by
       the roes and harts of the field do not stir up or awaken my
       beloved until it pleases her."

56.   What the Saint is saying, in effect, is that directors who err
       in this, even if they know no better (which is culpable), will
       have a lot to answer for. "He who recklessly errs will not escape
       a punishment corresponding to the harm caused—he is obliged
       in virtue of his office . . . not to be mistaken" (*text*).

57.   The Saint insists on the importance of recognizing one's own
       limitations in the matter of direction. Allowing, even advising,
       the person directed to find another director calls for true
       detachment and humility, recognizing "that it may have to
       change its mode and style of prayer and need a more sublime
       doctrine and another spirituality" (*text*).

58.   All depends on the director's recognizing that, having guided
       the soul in mortification and holy meditations, the time comes
       when God begins His special work, of contemplation, for which
       all else—the hammering, hewing, carving of the statue—was
       by way of preparation.

59.   St. John allows for the fact that one director may have all the
       qualities needed for the full direction of the soul, but he would
       think it presumptuous in a director to think he is qualified
       to direct all who come to him. Addressing them he says, "You
       tyrannize souls and deprive them of their freedom, and judge
       for yourself the scope of the Gospel teaching."

60.   St. John quotes from the well-known passage from Ezechiel,
       the "Parable of the Shepherds": "You have fed off their milk,
       worn their wool, and slaughtered the fatlings, but the sheep
       you have not pastured . . ."

61.   Directors should encourage freedom
        and advise souls to seek change if they feel dissatisfaction,
        as this might well be a sign of his inability to help,
        or that God is leading the soul by a different road.
        To act otherwise would be foolish pride and presumption.

62.   It can also happen that some directors,
        acting from human, selfish motives or from timidity,
        will actually put obstacles in the way
        and advise the soul to reject the inspirations of God,
        who is calling it to holy desires, renunciation,
        and conversion of life.
        This is completely in opposition to the demands of the Gospel.
        Instead of "compelling them to enter" (Luke 14:23)
        they compel them to stay outside.
        Whether these directors are aware or not
        that they are an obstacle to the guidance of the Holy Spirit,
        their conduct is culpable.

63.   The devil tries to intrude at this stage.
        The soul, infused with the delicate unctions of the Holy Spirit,
        has withdrawn in solitude from every other affection,
        and the devil tries to entice it
        to seek knowledge and sensible satisfaction
        with the temptation that it should be "doing something."
        Should this happen, God's work of drawing the soul to Himself
        is seriously impeded.

64.   The devil lies in wait to ensnare the soul,
        especially when it is passing over from sense to spirit.
        He achieves more damage
        through a little harm caused in these souls
        than by great damage done to many others.
        He feeds it with desire for things of sense, for ideas and
        knowledge,
        causing fear, anxiety, even bodily pains, strange sounds and
        noises.
        All too frequently he succeeds, and that easily,
        at the same time despising the soul
        for succumbing with so little resistance.
        Few are able to resist his wiles.

61. Ambition, foolish pride, presumption: these seem to be the besetting weaknesses of directors. Here one gains the impression that St. John's aggression toward spiritual directors is based on personal experience.

62. This paragraph contains perhaps the severest indictment of all. When it ought to be clear that God is calling the soul to higher things, the director, from unworthy motives—sometimes from fear of what, personally, is unknown—actually discourages the soul from following what is clearly the inspiration of God. Our Lord was very severe on "blind guides": "Woe to you, teachers of the Law, for you have taken away the key of knowledge and you neither enter yourselves nor do you allow others to enter" (Luke 11:52).

63. The devil is the second blind man, who being blind himself, wants the soul to be blind, too. He tries to deceive it with clouds of knowledge and sensible satisfactions. St. John warns us that many souls give in easily to this temptation. It is God who "provides solitude" and places the soul in it, "absorbing it to Himself by means of these solitary anointings."

64. St. John again insists on the importance to the devil of diverting the soul from entering into contemplation. In *The Spiritual Canticle* 40.3 we read: "Formerly he continually strove with all the armaments and force he could use to thwart the soul's entry into the fort of interior recollection with the Bridegroom." The devil enlightened souls to lose divine knowledge and he seizes and scatters the precious gold of the divine embellishments. See S.C.16 . 6: "The soul's protection is withdrawal into deep recollection in God."

65.   So the soul, greatly favored by God,
with silence and recollection
must give up the effort of laboring with the mind.
This activity, which was helpful in the beginning,
is now a serious obstacle and is to be abandoned,
not indeed by force but with detachment and freedom,
with simple, loving attentiveness to God
in peace and tranquillity.

66.   The third hindrance, or blind man, is the soul itself.
Being all too prone to revert to discursive acts,
it begins again the labor of performing them.
Instead of the enjoyment it experiences
in idleness, quiet, and silence,
it now becomes distracted, and filled with dryness and distaste.
It acts like a peevish child which kicks and cries,
wanting to walk when its mother wishes to carry him.

67.   Even though progress cannot be measured
in the state of solitude and quiet,
the soul is actually advancing much faster,
for it is God who is now carrying it along.
The thing to do is simply to abandon itself to God.

68.   We now return to the deep caverns of the soul,
the faculties—memory, understanding, and will—
which usually suffer intensely
when God is disposing sublime anointings of the Spirit,
drawing the soul into union with Himself.
The suffering arises from the very sweetness of these anointings,
causing the painful desire of unfulfilled longing.
How wonderful must be the fullness of possession
if these preparatory anointings of the Spirit are so sublime?

65.   Two points in this paragraph should be noted. (1) In the beginning, the activity and the use of the mind are necessary and important. St. John has been putting such stress on abandoning it that one could forget the need—that is, until such time as we are ready to enter into simplified recollection or, in St. John's terms, contemplation—for reflective meditation. (2) The "simple, loving attentiveness" which characterizes this form of contemplative prayer is indicated "when you feel no aversion to it." In *The Ascent* II.13 we read, "We take pleasure in being alone . . . we prefer to remain in general loving awareness of God."

66.   Left to ourselves, and lacking firm direction, we are all inclined to think we are doing nothing if we cannot actually assess progress or derive some satisfaction from what we achieve in prayer. In the very nature of God's action, it will be secret, not palpable to the senses, or the imagination, or the mind. So we tend to want to do our own thing, to go our own way, when God wants us simply to let Him carry us.

67.   This is the Saint's last word on the subject, as this is the last paragraph of the long digression which began in paragraph 27. The Saint now resumes his commentary on the "deep caverns of feeling".

68.   The apparent paradox of "sublime anointings of the Holy Spirit" and "intense suffering" is partially explained in paragraphs 18, 22, and 23 above (Stanza III). See also D.N. II:12.4: "Those to whom God's loving contemplation is communicated, must receive it according to their own capacity, which is limited, and in suffering . . . man being impure and weak, is ordinarily enlightened in darkness, that is, in distress and pain. Man must be spiritualized and refined in the fire of love; until then, he suffers trials and loving anxiety."

69.   It is through the faculties of memory, understanding, will,
that we have the power to taste God's communication of Himself
in wisdom and love; hence "deep caverns of feeling."
These three faculties minister to the power within us
of savoring the deep knowledge of God in His attributes,
just as sense-knowledge passes through the imagination,
which becomes a kind of archives
where sense impressions are stored.
In a similar way the three faculties minister to the soul,
which becomes the receptacle
for its experience of God's wisdom and excellence.

70.   *"once obscure and blind"*:

We distinguish between obscurity and blindness:
the soul is blind when it is in sin,
or gives way to wrongful desires;
if it is ignorant of supernatural things, it is in obscurity,
as it was ignorant of God's goodness
previous to God's enlightenment.

71.   One can be in obscurity, or ignorance,
without being in the darkness of sin.
Without God's illumination, the soul is in profound darkness
concerning the supernatural life.
Knowing only darkness, it prefers it to light;
but God, opening its eyes to the light of His grace
calls it even higher, to divine transformation
in which the light of the soul
and the light of God become one.

72.   Previously, the soul was not only ignorant but also blind—
blinded by its desires for gratification,
incapable of seeing the grandeurs of God's riches and beauty,
just as a cataract on the eye or even a small spot
will prevent clear perception of objects.

73.   So the clear vision of the knowledge of the things of God
is imperfect and distorted
by the gratification of natural-sense desires,
which are like the cataract,
clouding and blurring distinct vision.

69.   St. John refers again to the "lamps of fire"; it is through the
        "deep caverns of feeling" that they are experienced. In other
        words, the power given to us by God to "deeply experience
        and enjoy the grandeurs of God's wisdom and excellence" is
        exercised only through the memory, understanding, and will
        (explained in paras 19, 20 and 21 of this stanza). Sense-
        experiences are to the imagination (or phantasy) what the
        faculties are to this profound experience of God.

70.   "Once" means "in the past"—that is, before God intervened
        to enlighten and purify. In the blindness of sin, the soul cannot
        recognize its own ignorance. But by means of this transformation
        in God, it is illumined.

71.   It is not given to everybody to know the gift of God. Those
        who are not enlightened with God's special grace actually prefer
        the darkness, which they know, not recognizing the light.
        Cf. Jn. 3:19: "The light has come into the world, and men loved
        darkness rather than the light . . . everyone who loves evil hates
        the light, and does not come to the light . . . but he who does
        what is true comes to the light, that it may be clearly seen
        that his deeds have been wrought in God."

72.   "Any small desire or idle act in the soul suffices to hinder
        its vision of these great and divine things for which it longs"
        (*text*).

73.   The constant repetition in these paragraphs is evidence of
        St. John's desire to emphasize a basic principle: two contraries
        cannot coexist. Cf. *The Ascent* I.4: gratification of "self-indulgent
        affection without reference to God . . . is like darkness to His
        eyes. In such darkness, we lose our capacity to receive the
        pure, simple light of God."

74.   The unmortified desire for natural satisfaction
       causes a distorted view of spiritual things,
       so that they may seem of little value, or distasteful,
       or even appear as foolish.
       Even a desire for spiritual things
       may be purely natural.

75.   The longing for God is not always supernatural;
       it is only so when God infuses it,
       and only then has it any merit.
       To desire the pleasure of experiencing spiritual things
       is in itself merely natural—the act of one
       who lives simply for worldly desires and pleasure
       and is incapable of recognizing the supernatural.

76.   But now, since the bright and resplendent light of God
       has illlumined the soul in its deep caverns, the faculties,
       the darkness of its desires and affections
       gives way to the light of this divine union with God.

77.   "*with rare splendor,
         give warmth and light to the Beloved!*":

       Now that the caverns, the faculties,
       are marvellously infused with the wondrous splendors
       of those "lamps of fire" the attributes of God,
       they send back to God, in God, the Beloved,
       the same warmth and light that they receive,
       just as glass, struck by the sun,
       reflects back to the sun the splendor of its own light.

74.   It is easy to understand that a desire for some spiritual good,
       e.g. Heaven, may be purely natural. Some people desire to die,
       but as St. John says in *The Spiritual Canticle*, "this may be
       a natural imperfection." It may be a form of escapism.

75.   The Saint strongly asserts that true desire and longing for God
       can only come from God Himself, and only when God infuses
       it is it truly supernatural. So the longing we experience for
       God is itself a grace: "Long for the longing" (Tauler); "You
       would not be searching for Him, if you had not already found
       Him" (St. Gregory of Nyssa).

76.   What was once "obscure and blind" in the darkness of memory,
       understanding, and will—"the deep caverns"—is now illumined
       with the light of God Himself.

77.   It would be helpful to reread the Saint's commentary on "lamps
       of fire" (God's attributes shared with the soul), at paragraphs
       2–6, 14, 15, and 18–22 of this stanza (Stanza III). The simile
       is apt: the glass (the soul) struck by the light of the sun (God)
       reflects back the very same light that it received.

78.   "Rare" implies
         that the splendor is beyond description
         and its beauty cannot be exaggerated.
         For whether it be the understanding receiving divine wisdom,
         and becoming one with the understanding of God,
         or the will being united with His goodness,
         or with any of the divine attributes—
         fortitude, beauty, justice, etc.—
         the soul is, in a certain way, God by participation
         or, as it were, the shadow of God.
         So, even as God graciously gives Himself to the soul,
         the soul gives God in God to God Himself.
         For by God's gift "of hereditary possession"
         the soul has rightful ownership of God,
         who truly belongs to it, so that God and the soul
         mutually give themselves to each other.

79.   The soul experiences inestimable delight
         in this mutual exchange,
         realizing that it is giving to the Holy Spirit
         that which is its own.
         God accepts with gratitude,
         as though receiving something belonging to the soul.
         This reciprocal love is that of the surrender of marriage,
         in which there is a voluntary giving of self to the other,
         and the possessions of both, which are the divine Being,
         are likewise possessed by both together.
         All this comes to pass
         when God effects the transformation in the soul—
         not, however, as perfectly as happens in the life to come.

80.   The great satisfaction and delight of the soul
         consist in giving God more than it is worth in itself;
         this mutual love is always being renewed,
         in solitude, with the same divine light and warmth
         which He gives it—
         in this life, through the light of faith;
         in the next life, through the light of glory.
         So "the deep caverns of feeling", the faculties,
         with "exquisite splendor" give heat and light together—
         for the communication is that of Father, Son, and Holy Spirit.

78.   "Rare" is an attempt at rendering *extraños*—fifth line of the stanza: *con extraños primores*. The Peers translation renders it: "with strange brightness", and *Kavanaugh's* reads: "so rarely, so exquisitely". *Primor* may mean beauty or exquisiteness, or elegance. *Primores* literally means "splendors" (plural). We must remember that St. John is attempting to express the ineffable; language falls infinitely short of the reality—that we become "God, by participation." See also D.N. II.20.5, S.C. 36.5 and 39.4. The "rightful ownership" is by virtue of God's gift and initiative.

79.   These paragraphs should be read in the light of the seventeenth chapter of St. John's Gospel. St. John of the Cross quotes 17:10: "[Father] all I have is yours, and all you have is mine, and in them I am glorified." See S.C. 22.3: "Now begins the Spiritual Marriage . . . total transformation in the Beloved, in which each surrenders the entire possession of self with consummation in loving union."

80.   St. John speaks from experience. We read in his letters, "God communicates the mystery of the Trinity to this sinner in such a way that if His Majesty did not strengthen my weakness by a special help, it would be impossible for me to live." St. Teresa says, "All three Persons communicate themselves to the soul, and speak to it" (I.C. Mans. VII.1).

81.   As the soul experiences delightful enjoyment
        it presents this gift of God and of itself to God:
        exquisite love, praise, joy, gratitude.

82.   The soul now loves God,
      1. Not through itself, but through Himself;
        now it loves through the Holy Spirit
        even as the Father and the Son love each other.
      2. It also loves God in God,
        the soul being vehemently absorbed in God,
        and God in the soul.
      3. It also loves, not because God is good, glorious, generous,
        but because of who He is, in Himself, in His very being.

83.   There are three other kinds of splendor:
      1. The soul has enjoyment of God through God Himself,
        taking great delight in the distinct understanding
        of omnipotence, wisdom, goodness, and all His attributes.
      2. The soul delights in God alone,
        without intermingling of creatures.
      3. It enjoys Him for who He is alone,
        without intermingling of its own pleasure.

84.   There are three ways in which the soul praises God:
      1. As a duty, since for that purpose it was created.
      2. For the blessings it receives, and its delight in praise.
      3. For what God is in Himself, not for the delight it feels.

85.   There are three ways of gratitude:
      1. For the natural and spiritual blessings received.
      2. For the great delight it takes in praise.
      3. For praising God for what He is in Himself.

81.   Love, praise, joy, thanksgiving: from the beginning of the gift
       of contemplation, the soul realized that its praise and
       thanksgiving were gifts of God. The "exquisite" love etc. at this
       stage are the culmination; God is loving, praising, enjoying,
       thanking in the soul.

82.   Compare: "So that the love with which you loved me may be
       in them so that I may be in them" (Jn. 17:26). The mutual
       love of the Father and the Son is the Holy Spirit, Love-in-Person.
       Loving God in and for Himself alone, through the Holy Spirit,
       we love with the same love as the three Divine Persons for
       each other. Here is a reminder that while St. John of the Cross
       is speaking from experience, this makes real all that is founded
       in Scripture—that being baptized we become heirs to the
       Kingdom. The contemplative does not enter a realm that is
       alien, but turns back to the truth of existence.

83.   We now love, fully aware of our share in God's attributes in
       joyous delight. Like Jesus, we "exult in the Holy Spirit" (Luke
       10:21). In complete detachment, God's gift to us, we love God
       without any self-interest. Stanza 26 of *The Spiritual Canticle*
       commentary on "I no longer knew anything and lost the flock
       which I was following" describes how the Holy Spirit brings
       about this delight "in God alone, without intermingling of
       creatures."

84.   We are reminded that we were created for no other purpose
       than to praise God: "I have formed this people for myself; it
       shall sing my praises" (Is. 43:21). We come to the point of
       being praise and thanksgiving, like Elizabeth of the Trinity, who
       thought of herself as a "sacrifice of praise" and "a praise of
       glory."

85.   The "Magnificat" is the supreme expression of what St. John
       describes, the soul being "absorbed with great vehemence in
       praise", arriving finally at praise and thanksgiving "which is
       much more profound and delightful". The Blessed Virgin's life
       was a living, prolonged "Magnificat."

STANZA IV

How gently and lovingly
you awaken in my breast
where you dwell, secretly and alone!
And in your sweet breathing
filled with blessing and glory
how delicately you make me fall in love!

Commentary

1.   The soul turns to the Spouse with deep love,
       expressing its esteem and gratitude
       for two admirable effects which He sometimes produces
       by means of this union.

2.   The first effect is the awakening of God in the soul
       in gentleness and love.
       The second is the breathing of God within it
       through the blessings and glory communicated to it.

3.   So the stanza means:
       O Word and Spouse,
       how gentle and loving is your awakening
       in the deepest center of my soul
       where alone you dwell, in secrecy and silence,
       as its only Lord, as within my breast!
       And with what delicacy in this breathing of love
       you inspire me with love and affection!

4.   This awakening of God
       is that which brings the greatest good to the soul.
       It is a movement of the Word in the depths of the soul
       with such greatness, dominion, and glory
       that all the kingdoms of the world
       and all the powers of heaven are moved,
       as well as the perfections and graces of all created things.
       For when this great sovereign Emperor moves in the soul,
       all things in heaven, on earth, and under the earth
       move together, as one with Him.

1.   The "two admirable effects" are the subject of the remaining
      commentary.

2.   "Awakening" (used in all translations) is the rendering of the
      Spanish *recuerdo*. For the "breathing" of God in the soul, see
      S.C. 39.3–4. It is "the same 'spiration' of love that the Father
      breathes in the Son and the Son in the Father, which is the
      Holy Spirit Himself" (L.F. IV.17).

3.   Continuing Stanza 39.3 of *The Spiritual Canticle*—"There would
      not be a total transformation if the soul were not transformed
      in the three Persons of the Most Holy Trinity"—but here we
      are reminded that this grace is in and through the "Word and
      Spouse", Christ. Cf. S.C. 11.12: ". . . her Bridegroom, the Word,
      the Son of God, 'the splendor of His glory, the Image of His
      substance', Heb. 1:3."

4.   "The Word of God [is hidden] 'in the bosom of the Father' ".
      Now, in this divine awakening, the Word of God moves, or
      stirs, in the depths of the soul, which is "another Heaven"
      (St. Teresa). This is a movement, a stirring, of cosmic
      dimensions, as though "all balsams and fragrant spices and
      flowers of the world, mingling and shaken together, yield their
      sweet odor." The powers of heaven and earth are moved in
      this movement of the Word in the soul, and "all the virtues
      and perfections and graces of every created thing glow and
      move in unison" (*text*).

5.   And in moving they disclose
        the beauties of their being—power, loveliness, and graces.
        The soul realizes how all creatures of heaven and earth
        have their life, strength, and duration in God.
        It comes to know all created things better in themselves,
        knowing creatures through God, not God in creatures.

6.   Not that God moves; this only seems so to the soul,
        for all movement originates in God, the Prime Mover.
        It is the soul that is moved,
        "awakened" to the vision of the supernatural.

7.   The soul sees at once the very being of God
        and what He is in His creatures.
        It is as though a palace were thrown open,
        whereupon the eminence of the person within
        and, at the same time, what he is doing are revealed.
        God, as it were, removes the veils
        to reveal Himself as He really is,
        so that He can be seen, but partially.
        God seems to move in all things moved by His power.

8.   So lowly is our condition in life
        that we think others to be like ourselves.
        Thieves, and those given over to lust,
        think all others like themselves,
        while good people think only good of others.
        So, because we ourselves are careless
        and asleep in the presence of God,
        it seems to us that God is asleep, neglecting us,
        and thus we attribute to God
        what is characteristic of man.

9.   Our awakening is really an awakening of God,
        our rising is the rising of God,
        for God alone could awaken the soul from sleep.

5.   In Stanzas 4 and 5 of *The Spiritual Canticle* the soul "walks
        along the way of knowledge and consideration of creatures
        which leads to the knowledge of her Beloved, the Creator."
        Here, St. John quotes Romans 1:20: "The invisible things of
        God are known by the soul through creatures." Now all is
        changed; the effects are known through the cause, not the cause
        through the effects. We know creatures through God. This is
        a complete reversal of our first "discovery" of God in and through
        Creation.

6.   Although the "awakening" in Stanza IV, is attributed to God—
        "How gently . . . you awaken"—the awakening is really that of
        the soul. It is the newness of life in the soul which is the
        awakening, "since divine life and the being and harmony of
        every creature in that life, with its movements in God, are
        revealed in it in an entirely new way" (*text*). There is a movement
        and awakening of the soul from the natural vision to supernatural
        vision.

7.   This supernatural vision is a new and enlightened way of seeing
        into the very life and being of God, and of understanding how
        God moves, governs, and bestows being, power, graces, and
        gifts upon all creatures. It is as if a palace had been thrown
        open, to reveal not only what God is, but what He does. It
        is a removing of veils to reveal Him, but not totally, as happens
        in the next life, "so that we might see Him as He is" (*text*).

8.   St. John quotes Psalm 44:23: "Arise, Lord, why do you sleep?
        Arise!" But "He who watches over Israel never sleeps"
        (Ps. 121:4). We judge God according to our own petty, human
        notion of Him. It is we who are sleeping, perhaps neglectful
        and insensitive to the Holy Spirit's action "drawing us".

9.   Yet "only God can open our eyes and cause this awakening".
        So we pray for it: "Awaken and enlighten us, my Lord, that
        we might know and love the blessings which you ever place
        before us".

10.   This awakening is a communication of God's excellence
in the depths of the soul,
an immense powerful voice in the heart,
the voice of thousands upon thousands
of God's virtues and excellences.

11.   The question arises:
How can anyone endure so violent a communication
while in the weakness of the flesh?
In itself the soul has not the strength—
it will faint away, as Esther did,
at the mere presence of King Ahasuerus on his throne.

12.   The reasons it does not faint away are twofold.
First, being in the state of perfection
it is not subject to the pain
arising from purely spiritual communications,
a pain which arises from the impurity of the soul,
the lower nature not being conformed to the higher.
Second, and more important, God shows His gentleness
and loving-kindness proportionate to His power,
His dominion, His greatness.

13.   So God communicates His strength and His love,
going out to it from His throne,
touching it with His sceptre, embracing it.
The soul perceives the fragrance
of the wonderful virtues of God—
His charity, His knowledge—
in looking on the face of the Word,
and realizes that it stands like a queen
at the right hand of God.

10.   The Saint says: "What we know and experience of God in this awakening is entirely beyond description." The soul takes its place in the thousands upon thousands of God's infinite virtues and excellences, drawn up like an army in battle array.

11.   Job says of this communication: "When we have heard scarcely an echo of His voice, who will be able to endure the greatness of His thunder?" (Jb. 26:4) and "I do not desire that He commune and deal with me with much strength lest He overwhelm me by the weight of His grandeur" (Jb. 23:6).

12.   St. John modifies his statement that "the soul does not feel the pain . . . commonly experienced by those indisposed to receive spiritual communications" by saying that there is suffering in the presence of such grandeur and glory "even though the sensory part may be very pure." But God deals gently with us: He strengthens us, He who "with His right hand strengthened Moses, so that His glory could be seen by him" (Ex. 33:32). Recall the opening lines of the stanza: "How gently and lovingly/You awaken in my breast."

13.   God's "throne" is the soul itself; He goes out "like the bridegroom from his bridal chamber" (Ps. 18:6). The face of the Word shines upon the queen, which is the soul. The soul is aware of being a queen because it is transformed in the attributes of the heavenly King. "The queen stood at the right in garments of gold and surrounded with variety" (Ps. 44:10).

14.   *"Where you dwell, secretly and alone!"*

   God dwells secretly in every soul
   and is hidden in the depths of their being,
   thus preserving them in existence.
   In some He dwells alone, in others not alone;
   in some contented, in some displeased;
   in some as a ruler in his house,
   in others as a stranger.
   It is in the soul with fewest desires
   that He dwells contented, and completely alone—
   here He rules and governs.
   The more the soul is withdrawn from affections
   the more secretly does the Beloved dwell in it
   and with a more intimate and closer embrace.
   To this secret place, the devil cannot enter in,
   nor can the understanding attain to it.
   But to the inmost being of the soul,
   He does not dwell secretly,
   for it is conscious of this intimate embrace within it,
   though not always: sometimes there is an awakening;
   sometimes He seems to be sleeping.
   So there is not the fullest,
   most perfect communication of love.

15.   O happy the soul that is ever conscious
   of God taking His rest and repose within it!
   How fitting that it should withdraw from all things,
   leave business matters behind, and live in deep tranquillity,
   lest anything, however small, or the slightest anxiety
   should disturb the indwelling presence of the Beloved!
   He is there, habitually,
   asleep in this embrace with His bride,
   and the soul, always aware, has habitual joy in Him,
   though not yet as in the glory of Heaven,
   which is an eternal awakening.

14.   The soul's longing for the fullness of God's presence, as
       expressed in Stanza 11 of *The Spiritual Canticle*—"Reveal your
       presence"—has now been realized. This paragraph is St. John's
       summary of his teaching on the three kinds of presence:
       presence by essence, presence by grace, presence by spiritual
       affection (S.C. 11.3). This does not mean that God becomes
       progressively "more present" to us; rather we become more
       and more consciously aware of His presence as we become
       purified from affections and desires that are not of God. We
       have to remain concealed, and conceal ourselves in order to
       encounter and experience Him . . . "in hiding . . . in a way
       transcending all language and feeling" (S.C. 1.9). See also *Dark
       Night* 11, 12, 13, for the explanation of "secretly." The experience
       of God's presence becomes habitual, uninterrupted. In this life,
       there is always a certain "hiddenness" ("in darkness and
       concealment") but with "awakenings"—direct communica-
       tions, wholly divine and sovereign;substantial touches between
       God and the soul (D.N. II.11).

15.   "How fitting that [the soul] should withdraw from all things"—
       but not always possible! "Of course," St. Teresa says in *The
       Foundations*, chapter 5, "solitude is best, but charity or
       obedience may require you elsewhere." This question of
       "withdrawal from business affairs" is dealt with in *The Spiritual
       Canticle* 29 at some length. The extreme position taken by
       St. John—"Great wrong would be done to a person who
       possesses some of this solitary love . . . if we should urge him
       to be occupied in exterior or active things, even if the works
       are very important and demand only a short time"—arises from
       his anxiety that nothing should prevent this most precious grace.
       "One thing is necessary", Jesus said to Martha. St. John says,
       "O, how much could be written on this subject!"

16.   He dwells secretly, too, in others—those in grace—
        but these are not conscious of His presence
        unless He brings about certain awakenings in them,
        an awakening which is totally different
        from those of the perfect.
        These awakenings, inasmuch as sense enters in,
        are not secret,
        either from the understanding or the devil;
        the soul is not yet completely spiritualized.
        But in the awakening of the fully purified soul
        it becomes aware of exquisite delight
        of the breathing of the Holy Spirit in God,
        in whom it is glorified and enkindled in love.
        Therefore it says:

17.   *"And in your sweet breathing*
          Filled with blessing and glory
          How delicately you make me fall in love!":

        Of that breathing of God, full of blessing and glory,
        and of God's delicate love for the soul
        I do not wish to speak,
        for anything I should say
        would fall far short of the reality.
        It is a breathing of God Himself into the soul
        wherein the Holy Spirit breathes into the soul
        according to its understanding and knowledge of God,
        who profoundly absorbs it in the Holy Spirit,
        in whom it loves with a divine excellence,
        filling it with blessings and glory
        and a love for Himself transcending all description—
        a love in the deep things of God,
        to whom will be honor and glory for ever and ever. AMEN.

16.   This is the indwelling presence of God which is known by
        faith alone to those "in grace." The special "mystical" grace
        is that of the Holy Spirit giving us experiential knowledge, or
        felt awareness, of this presence, bringing about "certain
        awakenings" in which the soul is sovereignly glorified in the
        Holy Spirit of God. We begin to understand St. John's Gospel:
        "I have given them the glory you gave to me" (Jn. 17:22).

17.   Of this breathing, or "spiration", we read in S.C. 39:3 that it
        is so sublime and deep a delight that a mortal tongue finds
        it indescribable, nor can the human intellect in any way grasp
        it. "God sent the Spirit of His Son into your hearts, calling to
        the Father" (Gal. 4:6). In the second story of Creation
        (Gen. 2) we read that the Lord God breathed into man His
        own divine breath of life, and man became a living being. Now
        the transformation in God begun in baptism is complete, as
        perfect as is possible in this life, "transformed in the three
        Persons of the Holy Trinity in an open and manifest degree"
        (S.C. 39.3). By this divine breath-like "spiration", the Holy Spirit
        elevates the soul sublimely and makes it capable of breathing
        in God the same "spiration" of love that the Father breathes
        in the Son, and the Son in the Father, which is the Holy Spirit
        Himself, who is the Living Flame of Love.

BIOGRAPHICAL NOTE
St. John of the Cross

St. John of the Cross was born in 1542 at Fontiveros, a small town about twenty miles from Avila, the birthplace of St. Teresa. His father, Gonzalo de Yepes, of a noble family, had been disinherited when he married a poor silk-weaver, Catalina Alvarez. Shortly after John's birth, his father died, and his mother sought the assistance of her late husband's relatives. They treated her unkindly and refused financial help; the poor widow moved to Arevalo with John and his elder brother, Francis. From there they moved to Medina, the great market center of all Spain, but Catalina's efforts to support the family by weaving brought little income and she was forced to place John in an orphanage, where he remained until the age of 17. He was unsuccessful in learning a trade, and finally the administrator of the local hospital, noting his charity for the poor and his diligence in collecting alms, offered him a post as a male nurse. He carried out his duties well. At this time he was admitted to attend classes at the Jesuit college nearby, and without detriment to his work in the hospital he studied at night and successfully completed a four-year course of studies.

He was now 21, and his thoughts turned to the religious life. He asked for admittance to the Carmelite Order and was accepted, spending a year in the monastery before proceeding to Salamanca University, where he spent three years, being ordained as a Carmelite priest in 1567, at the age of 25. He returned to Medina del Campo, and his mother, brother, and sister-in-law assisted at his first Mass.

A few months later, he was introduced to St. Teresa, who in 1562 had founded the first house of the Discalced Carmelite Reform for nuns at St. Joseph's, Avila. She had received permission from the General of the Carmelite Order to found similar houses of the strict observance of the Primitive Rule of Carmel among the Carmelite friars. As it happened, John too was seeking a stricter form of life, and hoped to join the Carthusians. St. Teresa persuaded him to join the Reform, and he agreed, on the condition that the first foundation be made without delay. In November of that year he returned to the University of Salamanca, where he took a year's course in theology. He then returned to Medina del Campo, and accompanied St. Teresa to Valladolid, where a foundation of the Discalced Nuns had been made. He remained for some months, learning the ways and customs of the nuns with the help of St. Teresa.

After returning to Avila, he proceeded to Duruelo, a small, out-of-the-way village some thirty miles away. He was accompanied by a lay-brother, and they prepared the small farmhouse there, a gift from a gentleman from Avila, with a view to making the first Discalced

Carmelite foundation for friars of the Order. The house, poor as it was, was officially declared a Discalced Carmelite Monastery by the Father Provincial on the First Sunday of Advent, 1568. The first Community, of five members, lived there very austerely and with fruitful apostolate to the local people for a year and a half, after which they moved to a more spacious residence in Pastrana, a hundred miles distant. From Pastrana, a third foundation was made at Alcala, an important university city, with St. John of the Cross as first Superior. After one year, a request came from St. Teresa for John of the Cross to act as spiritual director to the Convent of the Incarnation at Avila, where Teresa, against her wishes, had been appointed Prioress.

A fruitful period of spiritual direction followed, and a valuable association with St. Teresa for two years. He accompanied her to Segovia, then on his return took up his duties as confessor. During this time, misunderstanding arose with the Fathers of the Carmelite Order whom John had left to enter the Reform. John was imprisoned at Medina del Campo; he was regarded as a disobedient religious, and there was not a little resentment over the success of the Reform. It is impossible for us to asses the real situation or to make a judgement regarding the motives of the people concerned. John of the Cross, freed at the intervention of the Papal Nuncio, in December 1576, was shortly afterwards carried off by force to the Carmelite priory at Toledo and imprisoned there, in a small, dark cell, enduring great suffering, until on August 16 of the following year he escaped. During those nine months he composed thirty-one stanzas of *The Spiritual Canticle*.

Following the meeting of the Discalced superiors at Almodovar in 1578 he was sent to the monastery of the Discalced Fathers in El Calvario, Andalusia, southern Spain. During this time he wrote the prose commentaries entitled *The Ascent of Mount Carmel* and *The Spiritual Canticle*. Except for short periods he was to remain in Andalusia for the rest of his life.

There followed appointments to the monasteries of Baeza, as Rector of the College, and Los Martires, Granada, as Prior of the house and Third Definitor. In November of 1581 he met St. Teresa for the last time, in Avila; she died in October of the following year. From 1582 to 1588 he was mainly at Granada, with occasional visits to the Carmelite convent at Beas. During this time he wrote the last stanzas of *The Spiritual Canticle, The Living Flame of Love* and other poems; the Commentary on *The Spiritual Canticle* (Second Redaction) and the Commentary on *The Living Flame of Love*. It seems that he wrote nothing of importance in the last five years of his life.

He became Vicar-Provincial of Andalusia and made five new foundations. Re-elected Prior of Granada, in 1587, he was chosen to attend the first Chapter-General of the Reform in Madrid, and was elected First Definitor and Consultor. In the same year he became

Prior of Segovia, in Castile, the central home of the Reform. He was re-elected First Definitor at the extra-ordinary General Chapter at Madrid, but he fell into disfavor with the General of the Discalced, Fr. Nicholas Doria. He was deprived of his offices, and the decision was taken, but afterwards revoked, to send him to Mexico. Instead he was sent to the isolated monastery of La Penuela, in Andalusia. His health was failing, and he went to Ubeda for medical aid, but ten weeks later he died, after much suffering, at midnight on Saturday, the eve of the Feast of the Immaculate Conception, 1591. His body was laid to rest in Segovia.

John was beatified by Clement X in 1675, canonized by Benedict XIII in 1736, and declared Doctor of the Universal Church by Pius XI in 1926.